IFR *for* VFR
Pilots

Also by Richard L. Taylor

Understanding Flying
Positive Flying (with William Guinther)
Instrument Flying
Fair-Weather Flying
Recreational Flying
The First Flight
The First Transcontinental Air Service
The First Flight Across the United States
The First Solo Flight Around the World
The First Human-Powered Flight
The First Solo Transatlantic Flight
The First Supersonic Flight
The First Unrefueled Flight Around the World

IFR *for* VFR Pilots

2nd / Edition

An Exercise in Survival

Richard L. Taylor

Aviation Supplies & Academics, Inc.
Newcastle, Washington

IFR for VFR Pilots; An Exercise in Survival
by Richard L. Taylor

Aviation Supplies & Academics, Inc.
7005 132nd Place SE • Newcastle, Washington 98059-3153
(425) 235-1500
Email: asa@asa2fly.com
Internet: www.asa2fly.com

Published 1997 by Aviation Supplies & Academics, Inc.
Hardcover edition published 1992 by Thomasson-Grant, Inc.

Printed in the United States of America

2012   2011   2010   2009   2008   9   8   7   6   5   4   3

ASA-IFR-VFR
ISBN 1-56027-280-5
    978-1-56027-280-9

Library of Congress Cataloging-in-Publication Data:

Taylor, Richard L.
    IFR for VFR pilots: an exercise in survival / Richard L. Taylor.
        p. cm
    "An Eleanor Friede book."
    Originally published: New York, N.Y.: Delacorte Press/E. Friede, 1982.
    Includes index.
    ISBN 1-5G566-004-8
    1. Instrument flying. I. Title.
TL711.B6T387 1992
629.132'5214—dc20   91-47532
                                          CIP

There are three parties to whom this book is dedicated:

First, to Eleanor Friede, editor and fellow pilot, whose insistence that the book needed to be written was the driving force in its completion...

Second, to those unfortunate pilots whose misadventures in instrument conditions provided much of the knowledge on which to base the procedures and techniques in the book...

Third, to those pilots who may benefit from realizing, accepting, and operating within their personal limitations. Long may they live.

Richard L. Taylor

I wish to acknowledge the work of Paul Haynie, several of whose drawings from an earlier book, *Understanding Flying*, help to illustrate some points which words alone cannot describe; Dr. Jerald Cockrell for his contribution of the chapter "The Human Element"; and the Macmillan Publishing Company for their permission to use the chapter "Why Not Get an Instrument Rating?" which appeared in the first edition of *Fair-Weather Flying*.

Richard L. Taylor

Contents

Author's Introduction

It used to be that a speaker could get a laugh from an audience of pilots by quoting one of the oldest lines in the business: "There are only two kinds of pilots—those who *have* gotten lost, and those who *will!*" Today that old saw has been expanded to cover landing at the wrong airport, landing with the gear up, groundlooping, and any number of embarrassing situations, and the best you can hope for now is a polite giggle. Pilots have heard it so often, or take their incident-free aviation experience so much for granted, that the venerable "two kinds of pilots" has been joined by a third—"it can't happen to me."

But it does, of course, and in all segments of aviation (military and air carrier pilots included). A lot of metal is bent and many egos are severely bruised as a result of the inattention, or lack of discipline, or lapse of common sense that is usually at the root of such mishaps.

At the risk of being accused of beating a dead horse, I'm going to nominate yet another candidate for membership in the wrong airport/gear-up/groundloop group, but I'm going to qualify it a bit: There are two kinds of VFR-only pilots—those who *have* flown inadvertently into instrument conditions, and those who *probably* will. This is not an idly conceived nomination; it's supported by the annual evidence, that recurring and continually disturbing set of statistics which shows that we haven't learned our lessons about nonqualified pilots trying to fly in weather conditions which deprive them of outside visual clues. These unhappy numbers are swelled, I think, by the panelful of instruments on most of today's training aircraft (let's face it: a 152 or Cherokee or the like with an artificial horizon, turn indicator, vertical speed indicator and VOR receiver is, relatively, a panelful), the brief exposure to instrument flight during private-pilot training, and the complacence generated by abundant "tools" and a smattering of knowledge.

It's a pretty heady concoction, this, when the 20- or 30- or perhaps even 10-hour private-pilot-to-be comes home after a hooded session and—with justifiable pride—announces to all who will listen that he has not only flown again today, he has actually *flown* an airplane *without looking outside*! Depending on the flight instructor, that thrilling episode and perhaps one more short demonstration of the newfound skill during the checkride may be the last time a lot of pilots give any thought to their abilities to survive without visual access to the outside world. And then, one day (or night) when the string has been pulled out all the way, and the only thing that stands between life and death is the ability to control the aircraft with reference only to the flight instruments, the skill that's required has atrophied beyond recall.

It's one thing to do an acceptable job of keeping an airplane right side up, or turning to specific headings, or descending to assigned altitudes when you're flying in a training situation—you *know*, you have every assurance, that no matter how badly you might botch the job, the guy or gal in the right seat will (1) keep you from getting too far into trouble and (2) will take control and pull your chestnuts out of the fire if you happen to venture too close to the edge. But it's quite something else when your aeronautical situation turns to worms and the right seat is empty—or worse yet, occupied by a nonaviator who is not only no help but may well be more trouble than you need at a time like this. People do strange things when they are convinced that the next person they're going to meet is their maker.

But enough fire, enough brimstone. The problem is strictly physiological (confused signals from the body's sensory systems), all aviators are potential victims (the number of flight hours in the log book may increase, but the ability to tell up from down in the absence of visual clues never improves), and there are only two solutions: complete avoidance of weather conditions that will induce spatial disorientation, or enough instrument-flying skill to get out of a low-visibility situation if you do get there, for whatever reason. It is, quite simply put, a matter of *survival*.

Setting aside mechanical failures and midair collisions, the statistics compiled over years and years of aviation experience leave no doubt that pilots who are not trained to cope with the problems of very low visibility — i.e., instrument flight — have an abysmally low chance of surviving such an encounter. When your very survival is at stake, you need a lifesaver—knowledge or a procedure or a skill that will at least give you a fighting chance — and that's what this book is all about.

IFR for VFR Pilots is not intended to groom you for the instrument rating (although the fundamentals of IFR operations and techniques certainly won't stand in your way if you should decide to go for it), it's not intended to provide a means of skirting around the law when weather conditions are less than legal for visual flight, and it's not a panacea for every type of weather-related emergency that you might encounter.

So what is the "Exercise in Survival"? It's the most basic, grass roots, fundamental, down-home, garden-variety type of lifesaver, a backup flying technique to help see you through this unhappy situation. It's a way to buy some time while you contact Air Traffic Control for help, and when that happens, it's a means to an end — ATC's best efforts are worthless if you can't comply with instructions from the ground.

IFR for VFR Pilots is also an explanation of the types of weather that are most likely to grow fangs; it will tell you what to look for in a preflight weather briefing, what to listen for en route, and what to watch for from that finest of all weather observation stations — your cockpit. It will give you an elementary description of certain aerodynamic characteristics of light airplanes and will tell you what tendencies to expect in an instrument situation. You'll learn about the various types of assistance available and how to communicate and cooperate with Air Traffic Control.

In accordance with the emphasis on survival for VFR-only pilots, navigation suggestions are limited to use of the most basic radio equipment—a good communication set for radar assists, one VOR receiver, possibly a transponder—but no advanced procedures like ILS or ADF. This is a *fundamental* system to get you out of trouble.

The human element in all this (that's *you*) is a low-to-middle-time pilot flying a light airplane (one or two engines) with a standard instrument panel (artificial horizon, directional gyro, at least) and reasonably good communications equipment. It's assumed that the airplane and its accessories are in good repair, and that the emergency or predicament has been caused by weather, not a mechanical or electronic malfunction.

IFR for VFR Pilots will undoubtedly contribute to your overall flying skill, since the control techniques are just as applicable in good weather as bad. After all, the *airplane* doesn't know whether it's flying in clouds or sunshine. But the primary purpose is to provide a lifesaving method that will enable you to cope with confidence.

After expounding on the virtues of flying techniques in four previous books, I sincerely hope that this "how to" volume is the one you'll never need to put to the test.

The pilot in command is the only judge of his ability to survive in weather conditions he observes ahead of his aircraft. When a non-IFR pilot has been operating in safe weather conditions and subsequently — for whatever reason — finds himself involved in an untenable weather situation, the near-universal solution is a 180 — and a return to known, survivable conditions.

There is nothing so absolutely fundamental to a pilot as survival; and there is no objective that justifies the certain risk of an attempt to continue flight in adverse weather. **Survival is everything.**

1 / Rules, Regulations and Requirements

Have you ever considered what it would be like if the automotive industry and the users of its products were regulated as closely as airplane manufacturers and pilots? No doubt one of the first effects would be an astronomical increase in the price of cars, followed by a drastic reduction in the driving population—there are a *lot* of people who just couldn't qualify for certification as drivers.

That's not likely to happen; however, the thought of it emphasizes the point that aviation is probably the most regulated activity in which any of us can engage. The rules chafe at times, particularly when a pilot is hampered by his own lack of legal qualification, but there's some comfort in the realization that nearly all the aviation regulations were written with safety in mind; they are attempts to protect us from ourselves. In matters of proficiency, both initial and continuing, the regs demand at least a minimum standard of achievement; our aircraft are manufactured and inspected under a system that, if applied conscientiously, virtually guarantees safe, dependable machines; and when it comes to where and how to operate those machines, the regulations provide a wide margin of safety. This latter category is of most interest here, and what follows is a brief review of those rules which will keep you out of the trouble for which this "Exercise in Survival" was written.

IFR Country: The Boundary Lines

In recognition of certain built-in limitations of the human body and mind, the rule writers decreed that no one should attempt flight in low-visibility conditions until a prescribed amount of special flight training had been accomplished and a successful assimilation of the new skill demonstrated. This is the instrument rating, of course, and without it your general limitations are ceilings of 1,000 feet and visibilities of 3 miles; in weather conditions lower than these, there is not time to practice effectively the universal anticollision technique of see-and-avoid.

So that you shouldn't meet someone else coming around a cloud, there are further requirements that you remain at least 500 feet below, 1,000 feet above, and 2,000 feet horizontally away from all cloud formations. In Class G airspace you need only remain clear of clouds (distance is up to you) and be able to see 1 mile … legal maybe, but not smart.

When Class C or D airspace is established around an airport, the purpose is to provide a chunk of airspace in which IFR operations can proceed with a guarantee that the only aviators there in weather less than the basic 1,000 and 3 will be those with instrument clearances. The VFR pilot who blunders into Class C or D airspace in lousy weather is jeopardizing not only his own skin but others' as well. *Stay away from busy airports when the weather is less than good.*

The FAA bent its usually stiff regulatory backbone a number of years ago and established a special type of Air Traffic Control clearance just to accommodate those pilots who find it necessary to leave or enter Class C or D airspace when ceiling and/or visibility values are less than those required for VFR operations. Known appropriately enough as a "special VFR" clearance, it permits any pilot, regardless of his qualifications or his airplane's IFR equipment, to enter or leave this airspace, the sometimes dangerous caveat that once beyond the zone (or before reaching its border inbound) he could fly safely in whatever weather conditions prevailed. Some days, when you *know* that good weather exists beyond the limits of Class C or D airspace, a special VFR clearance is a very practical and efficient way to use the rules to your advantage, but the special has become a crutch for many pilots who are willing to bet that the weather will improve as they fly farther from the airport. If it does, great; if it *doesn't*, you have placed yourself in, at best, an uncomfortable position. Once you report "out of Class C (or D) airspace," the Air Traffic Control system returns its attention to its first priority, the separation of IFR traffic—and you will probably have to either fly around in unfavorable weather conditions close to the ground (and TV towers, and power lines, and all the other airplane snaggers which inhabit that part of the airspace) until the controllers have time to serve you, or declare an emergency in order to get back to the airport. Use the special VFR privilege with great care; if things are bad enough to require a special, think twice about going at all. (*N.b.* Special VFR clearances are available at night *only* to pilots with current instrument ratings and flying properly equipped aircraft.)

Pilot in Command, It's Your Move

The most significant cause of weather-related accidents in the non-instrument pilot population is characterized by the familiar statement "Continued VFR flight in adverse weather conditions." Despite the regulation that requires pilots to familiarize themselves with literally *all* the information about a flight before takeoff (and which has been construed to apply to en route information gathering as well), people still manage to fly themselves into weather they aren't prepared to handle. In such a situation, when you realize that you're somewhere you shouldn't be, reluctance to let someone know, to holler for help, to declare an emergency, bespeaks not only a shortage of common sense but a lack of knowledge of the regulations and those provisions which can work very much to your benefit. Right up front, in Part 91, second paragraph, the authors of the regulations made you, the pilot in command, responsible for the operation of the aircraft, and also—this is important—gave you full authority to do whatever you think is best to solve the problem. In other words, all the rules go out the window when the situation progresses to emergency status; it's not a good place to be, but you need to know that you have *really* become the master of your own destiny—the law says so.

An Ounce of Prevention

There *are* ways to develop an emergency reservoir of skill and knowledge, to be dipped into when the need arises. You've taken one of the first steps in this direction by getting inside the covers of this book, but there's more to be done. Be honest with yourself: the hood time you logged during private-pilot training was probably the last time you've put yourself through that wringer, right? If not, you are to be congratulated; and if so, you need to reestablish at least that bare minimum level of skill. Would you be able to fly your airplane out of trouble tomorrow if you found yourself in the clouds?

There's a flight instructor somewhere nearby who will be more than pleased to spend some time with you in actual weather conditions. You may have to hunt for both the CFI and the weather to accomplish this, but if you've *never* been at the controls inside a cloud, it's high time you had the experience. While there's no requirement in the regs for real-weather time (unfortunately, not even for the instrument rating), an instrument instructor can see that you experience all the illusions, all the strange sensations of flight when you lose visual contact with the ground. A few such sessions should convince you that (1) you've no business even coming close to potential IFR conditions, and (2) if it *should* happen, all is not lost.

Until the *Real* Thing Comes Along

If you choose not to go the flight instructor route, there's still a way to develop and practice your IFR emergency skills well within the bounds of the regulations. You may *simulate* IFR conditions with an instrument hood of some kind, as long as the flight takes place in VFR conditions *and* the other pilot seat of your airplane is occupied by someone who is fully qualified to take over as pilot in command should the need arise. The law requires that the safety pilot be "appropriately rated," but your choice should go beyond that; this person is going to be your eyes outside the airplane as well as a potential rescuer if you happen to get the airplane into a compromising situation during your practice. Pick a good pilot, someone who is well qualified in the airplane, and in whom you are willing to place full responsibility for collision avoidance — with other planes, and the ground.

Without a doubt, the most difficult task you'll ever face in a weather emergency situation is the one in which all navigation is up to you—no radar, no DF steer, no help from another pilot, just you and the VOR receiver and bare minimum information from someone on the ground about radials, altitudes, and distances. Instead of hoping that you'll be able to handle it when the time comes, why not get in a little VOR navigation practice under controlled conditions? There's hardly a place in the United States where you can't find an out-of-the-way VOR and set up several different scenarios. Have your safety pilot play the part of the controller or FSS specialist, and see how close you can come to putting the airplane where you want it. Even if you miss by a country mile, you'll have added a bit to that emergency reservoir, and if it happens for real it won't be the first time. Baptism by fire is a sobering experience—if you survive. It doesn't need to be that way. Practice doesn't make perfect, but it sure helps.

With regard to the navigational facilities at larger airports—radar, direction finding equipment, etc.—you can prevail upon the folks in ATC to provide simulated emergency procedures when they aren't too busy handling the normal operations for which they're responsible. Particularly in the matter of radar "saves," controllers must conduct a certain number of radar approaches to remain qualified for the procedure, and they are generally happy to help you—and renew their currency—by going through a simulated emergency exercise. (Be certain that your request for any type of simulated procedure involving ATC is prefaced with the term *practice*.)

How Much is Enough?

One more item, and I'll get off the soapbox. Any skill once acquired must be exercised or it will be lost, and this applies in spades to instrument flying. The illusions, the false sensations, the potential for doing the wrong thing at the wrong time, make this—an inadvertent encounter with weather—an arena which demands at least minimum skill and knowledge. There's a "touch" associated with instrument flying, and if you haven't used it for a long, long time, don't expect it to come booming through in a pinch. No one can specify how often you should practice flying under the hood, or what maneuvers you should work on when you do; the important thing is for you to realize that any practice will be of benefit. When you feel comfortable with what you're able to accomplish in simulated IFR conditions, when you are confident that you could fly your airplane through an unexpected bout with the clouds and have complete control of the outcome, that's when you've practiced enough.

The pilot in command is the only judge of his ability to survive in weather conditions he observes ahead of his aircraft. When a non-IFR pilot has been operating in safe weather conditions and subsequently—for whatever reason—finds himself involved in an untenable weather situation, the near-universal solution is a 180—and a return to known, survivable conditions.

There is nothing so absolutely fundamental to a pilot as survival; and there is no objective that justifies the certain risk of an attempt to continue flight in adverse weather.

Survival is everything.

2 / Spatial Disorientation, or Body, Why Do You Lie to Me?

Sometimes an aviation medical examiner will ask a pilot to close his eyes and stand on one foot, with arms outstretched, just to find out if there are major problems in the examinee's balance mechanism. But what you may not notice is that the doc will stand close by, ready to keep you from falling if the "leans" get too severe; he knows that nearly all of us lose our sense of balance very quickly when deprived of the sense of sight. (Some pilots, of course, are able to stand upright for astounding periods of time—they can also "grease" every landing, make good every ETA on a cross-country flight, and perhaps even walk on water.)

You shouldn't be upset if, within a few seconds, you are doing a good imitation of the Leaning Tower of Pisa, because the human organism just isn't built to handle itself well in the absence of visual clues. Your eyes tell you where you are in relation to whatever is around you and are probably the greatest single factor in keeping your balance.

The Anatomy of Confusion

But the visual sense is only part of the rather remarkable mechanism which continually answers the question "Which end is up?" As you move about in your normal world, there's a very definite "feel" of the position you are in at all times; body sense informs you of vertical and angular movements by virtue of changes in the pressure and tension on your tendons, ligaments, muscles, and joints. Unfortunately, this proprioceptive sense (how's *that* for a ten-dollar word!) was not engineered to detect or report on circular movement, and therein lies one of the unique problems of the aviator.

The third component of the human balance system is a set of rigid hollow tubes embedded deep inside each ear. Generally referred to as the semicircular canals, these tubes are filled with liquid and lined with tiny, upright hairs which are sensitive to even the slightest movement of the fluid. Whenever you move your head, the tube moves but the fluid tends to stay put—inertia, you know—and the hairs are bent in one direction or the other. It's much the same effect when you rotate a tumbler filled with water; the glass (semicircular canal) moves but the water (fluid inside the canal) doesn't ... at least not right away. (Put some ice cubes in the glass, and you'll see very readily how they— and the water they're floating in—remain relatively stationary during the initial rotation of the glass.)

Each of the hairs in the semicircular canals is connected to an extremely delicate circuit which senses very small movements of the fluid and sends signals to your brain which are interpreted as changes in position. The three semicircular canals are arranged so that there is one lying in each plane of rotation; one of the canals is activated when you move your head from side to side (as in "no"), another when you nod (as in "yes"), and the third when you move your head as if to put your ear on your shoulder.

When these inputs—vision, body sense, and the signals from the inner ear—are combined in flight, you have a very trustworthy indication of your position relative to Mother Earth. For example, when you roll your aircraft into a bank, you see the wings tilt, you sense the resultant turn by virtue of the semicircular canals, and you feel the pressure of centrifugal force. The inner ear and deep muscle senses are important in the overall accomplishment of the objective, *but the eye is the key:* without vision, the other senses begin to play devilish tricks.

Consider the water-filled tumbler once again; if you rotate it very slowly, the water will turn with the glass. The same thing happens to the fluid in your inner ears when the airplane is turned smoothly and at a slow rate; if you couldn't see the turn taking place, you wouldn't know what was going on. In other words, there's a threshold of rotational sensitivity. This is important, because it not only permits a slow

The inner ear

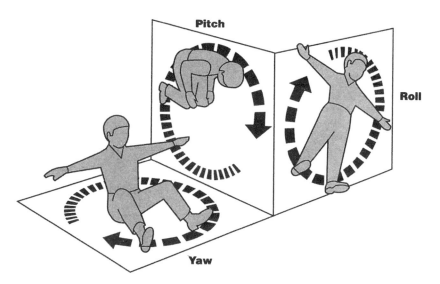

The semicircular canals and the three planes of rotation

turn to begin without your knowledge but may permit that turn to increase until the airplane is wrapped up in a really tight spiral—and you think you're still straight and level.

Yet another false sensation is generated when a turn is entered at a rate great enough to excite the inner-ear sense of rotation, but is then continued at the same rate. In this situation, the fluid in the canals bends the sensors as the turn begins, but inertia soon acts to

No Turn —
no sensation
True sensation

Top view of horizontal ear canal

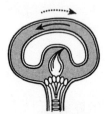

Accelerating Turn —
sensation of turning clockwise
True sensation

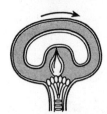

Prolonged Constant Turn —
no sensation of turning
False sensation

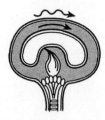

Decelerating Turn —
sensation of turning counterclockwise
False sensation

Sensations and the inner ear

slow and finally stop the fluid. The sensing hairs — with no turning force acting on them — resume their normal upright position, and your brain interprets the resultant signals as "straight ahead" — all while you are turning, turning, turning.

More on "Seeing is Believing"

Still not convinced that the inner ear can make a fool out of your sense of direction? Try this on for size: with eyes closed (and a safety pilot in the other seat), roll your airplane into a left turn at a rate that will definitely let you know what's happening, continue the turn until the fluid slows and stops (no sensation of turning now), then start rolling back to level flight. The fluid, which had stopped moving, will immediately provide a *right* turn signal to your brain, and if your objective is to keep the airplane flying straight ahead, you'll roll once again to the left to stop what you think is a right turn. And of course, that will result in an even steeper left bank. Quite literally, in this condition, you don't know what you are doing.

Keep in mind that these strange, uncomfortable, utterly false sensations are completely eliminated when you can *see* the natural horizon—when your eyes are able to confirm or deny what you feel.

But the problems don't stop with the inner ear; there are a lot of bad-news situations with regard to the proprioceptive sense, the feel of pressures and forces deep within your body. You are surely accustomed by now to the extra weight you feel during a steep turn, and it's quite likely that you have experienced the very same feeling when pulling out of a dive. Under normal circumstances (i.e., when you can *see* where you're going) your eyes tell you that all is well—that the forces you're feeling are the ones you expect to feel. And perhaps more important, there's no chance of misinterpreting those forces.

Now close your eyes and haul back on the wheel with enough force to pull a couple of Gs. Without vision to corroborate your feelings, *there is absolutely no way that you can distinguish a steep turn from a pullout*. Make the wrong decision when you move to correct the problem, and the fat's right back in the fire.

Now the *Bad* News...

So far, this scenario of confusion has considered a pilot sitting upright in the airplane, getting various inputs from the sensory organs during rather normal flight operations. No turbulence, no clouds, no concern for the safety of the airplane or yourself, because a quick glance at the outside world provides instant and reliable information about your

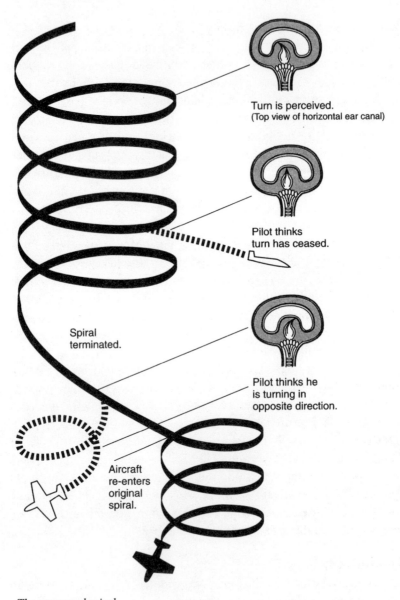

Turn is perceived.
(Top view of horizontal ear canal)

Pilot thinks
turn has ceased.

Spiral
terminated.

Pilot thinks he
is turning in
opposite direction.

Aircraft
re-enters
original
spiral.

The graveyard spiral

orientation with the earth. But remember that the semicircular canals are sensitive to *any* sort of rotation, and your deep muscle feelings will be triggered by *any* increase (or decrease) in gravity. Can you imagine the confusion inside your head if you should enter a turn while bending down looking for something on the floor of the cabin? Now the rotation is sensed by the canal that is normally in the *vertical* plane — you'll think that the airplane has pitched up (or down, as the case may be), and when you straighten up, a rotational sensation occurs for real in the pitch plane. Once again, it's easy to maintain control when you can see outside and recognize what's happening; you are able to override and ignore the false sensations because your eyes tell the truth.

If you should blunder into a cloud while looking for that chart on the floor, you are in for a big surprise when you straighten up and find nothing but gray where clouds and sky and horizon used to be. You'll know that something is wrong because it *feels* like the airplane is turning or climbing or diving or some combination of these, but without visual reference to the horizon, you have no foundation for taking corrective action. (If, in fact, corrective action is needed at all! What if the sensations you are experiencing have been induced by your own head movements, and the airplane is humming along in straight and level flight? The next untrained pilot who actually puts himself into this kind of trouble won't be the first one — not by a long shot.)

To really muddy the waters, throw in some turbulence, make it the middle of a dark night, and season the stew with a generous dose of uncertainty and genuine concern about getting this machine on the ground in one piece. When all these bad features of an unexpected weather encounter are added, the physiological forces are joined by a set of psychological problems — and the result is frequently more than the mind can handle.

Better Believe It

There is a lot more to be learned about the limitations and capabilities of the mind-body combination in circumstances such as these, but that's not the purpose here. This rather sketchy and oversimplified explanation of the physiological situation was put up front to convince you of the one inescapable fact that must become the backbone of your thinking throughout this book: without artificial visual clues to replace the natural horizon when it is lost to sight, *there's not a pilot alive who can maintain his orientation for more than a few seconds.* That statement includes veteran airline pilots, stunt fliers, everyone—we humans are just not designed for the task.

Equally important, since virtually all contemporary airplanes are equipped with the basic flight instruments, is the training to use the visual clues thus provided. What good are the instruments if you don't know how to interpret them and control the airplane by reference to their information?

The Only Alternative

It's such a crucial point that it needs to be said one more time: the human balance system cannot operate satisfactorily in the absence of visual clues, and spatial disorientation will occur in a very short period of time when those visual clues are lost. In order to fly successfully when there's nothing useful to be seen through the windows of your airplane, you must be trained to use the artificial clues provided by the flight instruments.

In the chapters that follow, there are techniques and procedures and special information to help the non-instrument rated pilot overcome these problems, but—here it comes again—there's no way around the flesh-and-blood simplicity of this fundamental point: you can't fly if you can't see outside and can't (or won't) use the artificial references provided on the instrument panel.

Okay, 'nuff said. Let's get to work.

The pilot in command is the only judge of his ability to survive in weather conditions he observes ahead of his aircraft. When a non-IFR pilot has been operating in safe weather conditions and subsequently—for whatever reason—finds himself involved in an untenable weather situation, the near-universal solution is a 180—and a return to known, survivable conditions.

There is nothing so absolutely fundamental to a pilot as survival; and there is no objective that justifies the certain risk of an attempt to continue flight in adverse weather. **Survival is everything.**

3 / *Weather to Watch Out For*

Strange as it may seem, it's not the violent weather that most often causes problems for non-IFR aviators. When the atmosphere is really churning, when thunderstorms and high winds and heavy rain or snow are doing their thing, most low-time pilots have the good sense—and perhaps the timidity—to leave the bird in the barn and wait for a better day, or to alter course and maintain a healthy distance from obvious cloud formations. Rather, the meteorological conditions which result in low stratus clouds, fog, multiple layers of clouds, and poor visibility in general are the conditions which most often "trap" unwary pilots. "Trap" in quotes because no mouse ever got caught without deliberately going after the cheese, and no pilot has been "trapped" by weather. Clouds don't appear out of nowhere and engulf an airplane; someone must fly the airplane into the clouds.

(Perhaps that last statement should be qualified a bit. In one circumstance—flying at night when a higher overcast shuts off moonlight and starlight—there's always the possibility that you can fly into a cloud which appeared "out of nowhere." But an adequate study of reports and forecasts, observation of the weather conditions before the sun went down, and careful attention to lights on the ground as you proceed, should provide enough clues to increase your awareness of the potential problem. In any event, such an encounter leaves you with the best of all weather penetration options; since you flew from clear air into the clouds, the most effective maneuver is the time-honored 180-degree turn, which will surely take you back to the clear air you just left.)

With the basic understanding that stratus clouds are the most likely troublemakers for non-IFR pilots, the problem can be further classified vertically. On the one hand, stratus clouds may form very close to or actually on the ground (fog), severely restricting or completely eliminating the airspace in which you can fly with visual ground contact; on the other hand, the pilot who flies above a solid layer of clouds must eventually penetrate those clouds in order to land. In either case, there's the unhappy probability that disorientation will occur, and it really doesn't matter whether it is induced by trying to fly under the clouds or over them.

The Principles Haven't Changed

The levels of the atmosphere with which we're concerned, i.e., up to about 10,000 feet MSL, contain varying amounts of moisture vapor—water in gaseous form. The problems begin to occur when some of that vapor becomes visible, creating clouds and restricting inflight visibility. The most frequent cause is the reduction of air temperature, and when it is lowered enough to cause condensation of the moisture vapor in the air, some sort of visibility restriction will become apparent. It's *haze* in its early stages, *clouds* when the condensed droplets get large enough to form an organized mass, and *rain* (or snow) if the droplets continue to grow.

Therefore, if you understand what meteorological phenomena are likely to provide the magic combination of moisture and temperature, you can do a good job of staying away from the conditions (existing or potential) which might get you into trouble. The variety of cloud-creating weather circumstances is not a large one; it can be limited, albeit simplistically, to (1) the action of weather fronts, and (2) the results of air-mass modification.

Weather in Action—the Frontal View

If air masses could be colored throughout—blue for cold air and red for warm—the theory of weather fronts could be proved or disproved. As it stands, there is little choice but to accept the meteorologists' theory that a zone of discontinuity exists between unlike air masses, and that they conflict along these boundary zones in a "battlefront" situation.

As air masses advance and retreat across the surface of the earth, the weather produced along the front can vary from disastrous to nothing at all. Changes in temperature, pressure, and humidity alter and affect the air on both sides of this meteorological war zone and generate clouds, wind, fog, precipitation—all the forms of weather known to man. In addition, there are some mechanical considerations involved with the movement of a front, because a bubble of high-pressure air muscles other air masses out of the way, with some of the displaced air inevitably being forced upward—expanding, cooling, forming clouds if there's enough moisture present. When you know something about the air masses involved—relative temperatures, pressures, and moisture content—it's possible to predict with at least a fair amount of confidence the type of weather to be expected where the air masses meet.

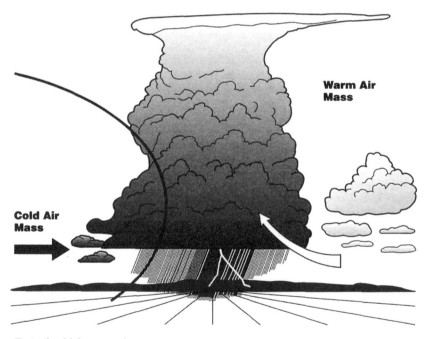

Warm Air Mass

Cold Air Mass

Typical cold-front weather

Based on prominent characteristics, there are four types of weather fronts—cold, warm, occluded, and stationary:

Cold Front: The leading edge of an advancing cold air mass, usually one with high pressure and density but relatively little moisture. As the leading edge of a bubble of air, the cold front forces great volumes of warmer air upward; the faster it moves, the more vertical (and more violent) weather it generates.

Warm Front: The leading edge of a rather flat wedge of retreating cold air. A warm front tends to be more subdued, but the associated weather extends over a much wider area than that produced by a cold front.

Occluded Front: The occluded front represents a mixture of both cold and warm frontal weather. It is produced when the cold front moves much more rapidly than the warm front, and either pushes the warm front aloft or rides up and over the sloping surface of the warm front.

Stationary Front: When any frontal system slows down or stops, the meteorologist classifies it as a stationary front. Since the energy of movement is no longer present to generate much weather activity, a stationary front is usually much less violent, and the weather conditions will be similar to those associated with a slow-moving warm front.

Low Visibility: The Working Ingredients
Each of these frontal types is capable of producing conditions of great concern to pilots who must avoid areas in which visibility is reduced below legal, safe values. Occluded fronts are relatively rare, and cold fronts *usually* produce vertically developed clouds which tend to draw moisture upward and render the lower levels of the atmosphere relatively clear. Therefore, warm fronts and stationary fronts have the potential of creating widespread persistent weather conditions which meet all the requirements for low visibility over very large areas. In both cases, the shallow slope of the frontal surface provides a wide band of stratus clouds often extending nearly to the ground, with considerable precipitation from these clouds into the cooler air below. In addition to the cooling effect of the air itself, some of the rain will evaporate as it falls, further lowering the temperature, and the released moisture will likely create even more cloudiness—bad omens for the non-IFR pilot.

After a front passes, weather conditions depend mostly on the moisture content of the air mass and the heating or cooling that may occur. A moist air mass over land of a lower temperature will be cooled from below, and you should expect low ceilings and visibilities, the degree of which will be a function of the dew point–temperature relationship. On the other hand, a moist but clear postfrontal air mass that is heated by the surface will likely produce localized cumulus clouds—"fair-weather cumulus"—and scattered thunderstorms when gross instability is present. When an air mass is very dry, look forward to fine, bright weather on the west side of the front.

In those areas where the atmosphere is not fouled by smokestack emissions and the inevitable byproducts of energy production, the crisp, clear air behind a cold front will exist for days—often until the next weather system moves through—but those conditions seldom exist around our large urban centers. Within a day or two after cold-frontal passage, man-made pollutants begin to cloud the clear skies and provide the nuclei for condensation. This is industrial modification of an air mass, and frequently creates low visibility in the form of a haze or smog layer that can extend upward for 10,000 feet or more above the surface. So far as pilots are concerned, the source of the restriction is immaterial—low visibility is low visibility is low visibility.

When an air mass comes to a standstill, it begins to take on the characteristics of temperature and humidity that exist on the surface. Significant modification can occur when an air mass remains over a

Typical warm-front weather

particular land or water area for an extended period of time. Moisture content may increase and temperature may rise or fall and provide a completely different set of results when the air mass is finally pushed out of the way by the next system.

The Weather Briefing, the Questions to Ask

Of particular interest then, to the non-IFR pilot, is a good preflight briefing which includes the type of weather along the route and the projected movement of those weather systems that may affect the flight. A briefing which mentions virtually any kind of frontal activity should get the attention of a VFR-limited pilot, because of the strong probability that moisture vapor will be condensing somewhere in the frontal zone, creating lowered visibilities. Assuming that a weather briefing will be obtained for every flight outside the local area (it's not only very good sense, it's required by the regulations—FAR 91.103), ask the specific question "Are there any frontal systems likely to affect my route of flight?" if that information is not volunteered. And when that request elicits the information that a *warm* front is in your flight area, be doubly concerned—dig deeper.

There's a wealth of information available, and a host of clues to the probability of your running into below-VFR-minimums conditions. Flight Service Station briefers (or, on occasion, National Weather Service forecasters in those situations when you cannot get in contact with an FSS) will normally include information from all these sources, especially if you identify yourself as a non-IFR pilot. But it behooves you to be aware of the pertinent products of the weather information system, so that you can ask intelligent questions during the briefing.

Preflight: The Weather Information at Hand

The most general source of aviation weather information is the *aviation area forecast*, with geographical coverage of at least several states. You'll find information about fronts and air masses, general cloud conditions including types, bases, and tops, and the amount of visibility expected to prevail throughout the forecast period. A most worthwhile portion of the area forecast is that devoted to precautionary statements, hazardous weather advisories. Mention of a SIGMET

(SIGnificant METeorological advisory) is enough to perk up the ears of *any* sensible aviator, airline captain and private pilot alike; SIG-METs refer to such nasty conditions as severe thunderstorms, hail, really heavy turbulence, and so on. But the VFR pilot's antennae should stand straight up when an AIRMET (AIRman METeorological advisory) appears in the area forecast; an AIRMET concerns weather conditions less severe than a SIGMET, but which may be hazardous to some aircraft (light, low-performance airplanes) *or to relatively inexperienced pilots.* The most significant feature of most AIR-METs is the reference to the onset of areas of visibility below 3 miles and/or ceilings less than 1,000 feet, including obscured mountain ridges and passes. As a catchall statement, whenever an AIRMET shows up, you must explore the situation further, because it's very likely that IFR skills will be required somewhere within the geographic area of that forecast.

Terminal aerodrome forecasts (TAFs), which cover the immediate environs of an airport, are also of considerable value in the decision-making process, if for no other reason than to confirm, for the airports along your route of flight, the conditions spelled out in the aviation area forecast. While the accuracy leaves something to be desired (remember that even with satellites and high-technology methods, forecasting is still very much an inexact science), you must consider any near- or below-minimum forecast with much more gravity than the IFR-rated pilot; *you* don't have the option of filing IFR if the forecast is in error on the bad side, or "busted," as they say in the weather business.

In addition to what's expected (forecasts and advisories), a good preflight briefing will include a rundown of *existing* weather along the route—the surface weather reports (METAR). With this information, you can verify the accuracy (or lack thereof) of the forecasts, and identify trends at the various reporting points. For example, if the forecasts indicate that airport A should remain well above VFR minimum until two hours after your arrival, but the report for the current hour shows that the ceiling is *already* approaching your tolerance, it's time to think seriously about plan B.

Where the Weather is—For Sure

One of the best clues available to predict the onset of low visibilities is the surface temperature-dew point spread, and its importance harks back to the fundamental principle of cloud formation: when the temperature of the air reaches a certain value — its dew point — condensation begins and tiny droplets of water thus suspended in the atmosphere produce first haze, then clouds, then precipitation if the droplets grow large enough.

Fortunately, this information is part of every weather report and is easy to interpret. The observed temperature is recorded in degrees Celsius, followed immediately in the report by the *calculated* dew point, also in degrees Celsius. The mixing and movement of layers of air close to the ground must be taken into account, and so it's not safe to wait until these two values reach equality to make the go–no go decision. As a rule of thumb, whenever the difference between surface temperature and dew point—the spread—is reported to be 2–3 degrees C, you must expect that low clouds will begin to form in the near future. It's true that there are other circumstances bearing on this condition, such as wind direction and velocity, characteristics of local terrain, and time of day, but the pilot who takes a closer look at the advisability of flying into an area of diminishing temperature–dew point spread is by far the wiser one. As the spread diminishes, your options are more than likely being reduced as well.

The Inflight Advantage

Once airborne on a VFR flight, you're in the catbird seat; the very best weather observations in the world are those taken from the cockpit. You can *see* the curtains of precipitation hanging from clouds ahead; you can *see* the walls of cumulus canyons closing in on all sides; and you can *see* terrain features and lights on the ground beginning to disappear as you fly into lowering visibility. When you can *see* weather conditions that are obviously going to require instrument skills and training, *don't press on;* things will almost invariably get worse before they improve.

A really clear day is known in the trade as CAVU—ceiling and visibility unlimited—the kind of day when you can see "clear into tomorrow"; but when the atmosphere begins to get clanked up with condensing moisture, dust, smoke, smog, etc., the limits of visibility shrink accordingly. In such a situation, you'll find yourself flying at the apex of a cone of visibility, the edges of which travel along in front, to all sides, and to the rear of your position. The faster you fly, the faster obstacles appear out of the murk, so one of the first things you should do when encountering these conditions is *slow down;* you'll be spreading events over a greater time period, which gives you more time to think and react.

Signposts to "IFR Ahead"

The nagging discomfort of flight in a low-visibility situation will be very apparent; you'll feel it in the pit of your stomach—"something isn't quite right here." And when the size of the cone is obviously getting smaller, there's a rule of thumb to confirm what you feel; look down at a 45-degree angle (halfway between straight out and straight down), and you'll be looking at something which is as far away from you as you are from the ground. For example, when you are flying at an altitude of 5,000 feet above the ground, a point that lies on the 45-degree line of sight is just about a mile away; if you look down only 30 degrees, the distance increases to approximately a mile and a half. Apply that rule to the altitude that might be required to remain clear of a low ceiling—say 1,000 feet AGL—and you've got to agree that *whenever* you notice that you're flying at the top of a gray cone, it's time to do something other than continue.

At night, lights are the major clues to deteriorating visibility; stars and moon above, ground lights below. When either begin to disappear, heed the warning; the only two things which could cause such a blackout are rising terrain or clouds, and contact with either is not conducive to longevity. Lights on the ground will exhibit very definite halos when the air is filled with moisture and is ripe for fog formation; you'll often see the fuzziness some time before the fog becomes apparent. When ground-light sources begin to appear "soft" instead of the usual sharp pinpoints, fly away from that area or get on the ground in short order—fog cannot be far behind.

En Route Weather Information

There are numerous sources of inflight weather information to help you stay abreast of the meteorological situation. For example, there are TWEBs—transcribed weather broadcasts—available on the audio channels of certain VOR transmitters, with reasonably current reports and forecasts for airports within 400 miles of the broadcasting location. When you approach a major terminal, the Automatic Terminal Information Service (ATIS) provides a frequently updated recording of conditions close to the airport.

Perhaps the very best source of en route information is a service established specifically for this purpose; it's known officially as EFAS—Enroute Flight Advisory Service—but more universally recognized in the aeronautical community as Flight Watch, the code phrase used to call one of these stations. You'll be talking to a Flight Service Station specialist, but one who does not deal in copying flight plans, preflight briefings, and other routine, ground-bound matters; *this* specialist has as his sole objective the communication of en route conditions—pilot reports, terminal aerodrome forecasts, hazardous weather advisories, and the like—to *airborne* pilots. There's a lot of help for the asking, and the asking is so easy.—just tune your communication radio to 122.0 and call "Flight Watch," followed by your call sign and approximate location. This service is normally available from 6:00 A.M. to 10:00 P.M. with near-total coverage of the United States at altitudes of 5,000 feet AGL and above.

One more weather situation which too often results in a VFR-limited pilot getting into serious trouble, a situation that has nothing to do with the usual stratus/fog condition. You'll *see* cumulus clouds building up along your route of flight, and normally they are easy to circumnavigate unless lines or solid areas have formed. But during the initial stages of this sort of buildup, it's very tempting to increase altitude (especially if you're at the helm of a high-powered or turbocharged airplane) and sail over the tops of the clouds that stand in your way. Be advised that in many cases cumulus clouds will build at a rate that exceeds the climb capability of your airplane (even the highest-powered general aviation machines), and when you turn around to fly away from that solid wall of white ahead, you discover that the buildups have closed off every avenue of escape. Even if you can continue to climb in clear air by circling, the oxygen problem will rear its ugly head sooner or later, and the airplane's climb rate will diminish steadily, to say nothing of the probability that the floor of your "hole in the clouds" will rise relentlessly under you. Flying over the top of a well-defined stratus layer is chancy enough, but trying to top an area of active, building cumulus is folly indeed; such a maneuver is truly "going after the cheese."

The Winning Combination

There should be no flight so important, no trip so urgent, that it can't be postponed if unfavorable weather conditions appear. Given the wealth of information available prior to a flight, the weather reports, forecasts, and advisories that are yours for the price of a simple radio call or a few moments listening after you're airborne, *and the unexcelled accuracy and dependability of your own in-cockpit observations*, there is no reason why you should ever find yourself "trapped" in weather conditions which require skills you don't possess.

The pilot in command is the only judge of his ability to survive in weather conditions he observes ahead of his aircraft. When a non-IFR pilot has been operating in safe weather conditions and subsequently — for whatever reason — finds himself involved in an untenable weather situation, the near-universal solution is a 180 — and a return to known, survivable conditions.

There is nothing so absolutely fundamental to a pilot as survival; and there is no objective that justifies the certain risk of an attempt to continue flight in adverse weather.

Survival is everything.

4 / *Communicating*

Funny thing about pilots. They'll fly themselves right into the middle of a truly dangerous situation and *then* think of calling somebody — *any*body! — for help. And the call usually falls into one of two categories: a frantic, pleading cry for help, or a calm announcement that "we've, ah, flown into some clouds here, ah, looks like I'm gonna need radar vectors to Podunk." There are shades of gray, of course, and the accident/incident reports are filled with a wide variety of pilot declarations of impending or actual emergencies.

Funny thing about controllers, too. Whether they're sitting in front of a radarscope in an Air Route Traffic Control Center, working in the cab of a control tower, or going about their business in a Flight Service Station, they may respond to the call of a pilot in trouble in as many different ways as there are personalities involved. Some handle such a situation very well, some get off on the wrong foot with the first word; that's human nature, and there's not much to be done about it.

But the type of response is not especially that of the controllers; it's the timing that's important. Whatever the reasons, pilots seem very reluctant to declare an emergency until they are in the thick of it — and frequently, when it's too late for anyone on the ground to help them.

This frame of mind shows up every now and then on a check-ride. When the examiner simulates engine failure on a single-engine airplane, it's not at all uncommon for a pilot to go through the initial steps of his emergency procedure, then, while gliding down to the field he has picked, say something like "... and of course I'd call the tower and tell them I'm landing in a field about 8 miles north." Nothing wrong with that, but there is no possible assistance forthcoming from the tower controller. Perhaps there's a feeling that the fault in this situation is not human, but mechanical, and therefore an admission of trouble carries no stigma, no hint of error on the part of the pilot. Apparently "I've lost my engine" is a lot easier to say over the radio than "I've lost my way."

Now, Just in Case ... The Pre-Emergency Contact

Timely communication of your concern for what lies ahead is of the utmost importance, for it gives the people on the ground the opportunity to look over the weather information and advise you of the best options available. At the very least, a call to the nearest Air Traffic Control facility establishes a line of communications, and if all the doors close around you, the first step in getting out of the difficulty has already been taken.

The most likely contact in such a pre-emergency situation would be the ATC facility you're working with at the time; a Flight Service Station, "Center" if you happen to be taking advantage of their radar advisory services en route, a control tower or approach controller if you are operating in close proximity to an airport. A report of weather conditions in the general area in which you're flying goes a long way in determining which way to turn toward a safe haven (if the controller you're working with at the time doesn't have the information readily available, he'll give you the frequency for someone who *does* have what you need).

At this point it should be necessary only to inform whomever you contact that you have some doubts about continuing safely in the weather conditions you observe; no fancy code words needed, nothing more than plain-language declaration of your concern. The important thing is not how, or with whom, but *when*. Do it *now!* This is not a declaration of an emergency, but an information-gathering process, a means of confirming what you suspect about the weather ahead; of course, when you have been flying in conditions which are tenable for you and are confronted with conditions you *know* you cannot handle, the only smart thing to do is the ever-popular 180.

Now! 'Fess Up and Declare!

Let's carry this one step further. Assume that you have strong doubts about continuing in VFR conditions, the weather reports you have received confirm that things are not getting any better up ahead, and it appears that the weather may even be closing in behind as well. You are now treading a very thin line between success and failure, and it is time to communicate *positively* with someone on the ground. This should be no information solicitation—you've already done that—this should be a bona fide declaration of your situation and a call for help; it's free for the asking.

Much is made of the code words that pilots are expected to use when declaring an emergency, and there's no doubt that whenever the speakers in a Flight Service Station or tower or Center come alive with "Pan, pan, pan!" all the controllers will pay attention to whatever follows. Even more strident and attention-getting, of course, is the international distress code word, "Mayday, Mayday, Mayday!" (from the French *m'aidez*, "help me"). But it's not necessary to be all that dramatic in the predicament under consideration here, nor is it necessary to make a determination of whether your problem is of an urgent nature (in which case, saith the book, you should use "pan"), or one that requires the use of Mayday (in other words, a condition of true distress). A simple statement of the problem will suffice: "Center, this is Piper 1234, I've flown into some clouds, I'm not instrument-rated, and I need some help to return to VFR conditions."

You can bet your life's savings that such a transmission will bring an immediate response, especially if you let Center know some time ago that this might happen. (When you've been flying without benefit of radio contact with anyone, when no one in the area knows that you're aloft, your "I'm in trouble" message needs more punch, something to make it stand out in the crowd of routine air-to-ground transmissions. Here's when you can and should use "Mayday!" to get prompt and preferential service.)

And, in a Communications Crunch...

The ability to communicate your plight on an established frequency to someone with whom you've been talking underscores again the importance of a "pre-emergency" call. But whenever you've been out of contact, or are not at all sure whom to call, there's an easily remembered, works-every-time solution: merely tune your communications radio to 121.5 MHz, the international emergency frequency, and say "Mayday, Mayday, Mayday, any station reading Piper 1234, please reply; this is an emergency." If everyone is minding his aeronautical manners, the *only* messages on this frequency will be of a distress nature, and ground stations will respond promptly. Most ATC facilities and military air installations monitor 121.5 at all times. If there's anything for sure in this world, it's the near certainty that a distress call on 121.5 will be heard by someone in the system. Remember that, like any VFR transmission, range will be limited to line of sight; your altitude will probably be the ultimate determiner of how far away your message will be heard. If it's practical and possible for you to climb, do so; every foot of altitude improves your ability to communicate.

The Controllers' Need to Know

The stigma of officially and publicly declaring an emergency is partly taken out of your hands by the discretionary powers granted to ATC controllers. When one of them judges that the situation you have described over the air is indeed one that should be treated as an emergency, that's exactly what takes place, and all the protective and helpful wheels begin to turn, probably without your knowledge. In any event, whether the emergency is pilot-declared or controller-determined, there are certain pieces of information required by the ground station. You should be prepared to tell them the nature of the problem, the weather conditions in which you're flying, your intentions, and what you'd like them to do for you. Provide your present position, if you know it; if you're lost, it's helpful to give ATC the last known position, when you were there, and what heading you have been flying since that time. Your altitude is important, as is — to some extent, at least — the number of people on board the aircraft, and any other information that might prove helpful; this latter will vary with location and situation.

As the controller or FSS specialist goes down his checklist of information to be obtained from a pilot in trouble, he'll eventually come to the item labeled Fuel Remaining—pretty important so that he'll know how much time he has to work with you. The only meaningful answer to the question about fuel remaining is, of course, the amount of *time* left in your tanks. There's an old story about an inexperienced pilot who got into trouble, contacted a Flight Service Station for help, and when the specialist said "Say fuel on board," remained silent. Another request from the FSS brought no response. Finally, on the third try, "Say fuel on board" was answered with "Texaco."

Whatever the predicament, no matter whom you're talking with on the ground, there's no need for you to bother your brain trying to supply *all* the information; that's what checklists are for, and you can rest assured that the controller will elicit whatever is needed. If any of the requests appear to be taxing your concentration and division of attention to the point of affecting your ability to control the airplane, let the controller know—there's time for question answering later on. *Fly the airplane!*

The Machinery in Motion

An unseen, unheard sequence of events is placed into motion when the first facility receives your notification of an impending or actual emergency. Controllers will begin cross-checking with each other to locate you, downstream controllers are alerted to the possibility of picking up your target on their radarscopes, supervisors begin to assign duties to optimize manpower, and the communications network begins to hum with inquiries about weather conditions throughout the area. In order to provide you with the best possible service in an emergency, controllers and specialists need as much lead time as possible; give them a better chance to help by transmitting your plight as soon as possible. Again, the "pre-emergency" call may well be the most important.

First Things First

If personal pride or embarrassment is the leading factor in the reluctance of pilots to actually declare an emergency, fear of having to submit a formal report to the authorities must surely run a close second.

You should take great comfort in the latitude the Federal Aviation Regulations provide in this area; FAR 91.3 not only invests you with the responsibility for the conduct of a flight but also gives you the *final authority* on the operation of the aircraft. In other words, the rule writers recognize that there's usually no one in a better position than the pilot to determine what's best for the situation. Part 91.3 gives you official authority to deviate from any of the rules of the air to the extent required to meet an emergency.

Worried about writing a report after it's all over? That's a concern not worthy of your time right now; anyway, you must file a report *only* if it's requested by the administrator (through one of his agents, of course), and it's more likely that you'll wind up talking it out with an FAA inspector. If everybody lives happily ever after, a report (oral or written) is a small price for surviving. Pay it gladly.

In summary, consider the following with regard to communicating in an emergency:

- Let someone know just as soon as you suspect an impending problem. The earlier the better.

- Don't be hesitant to declare an emergency—there's no better way to marshal the services available to help you out of trouble.

- Know that "Mayday" is the international distress code word, and that use of it on the air will get an immediate response.

- Cement this number in your mind: 121.5. It's the international distress frequency, and you are virtually assured of a response when you use it to announce an emergency. Don't change to 121.5 if you are already in contact with ATC.

- Remember that you, the pilot in command, have the final authority for doing whatever you think is best at the time—even if it involves a deviation from the Federal Aviation Regulations.

- Don't be concerned about the possibility of having to file a report with the FAA after the situation has been resolved. Unless your discretion was a flagrant violation, the chances are good that the inspectors will see to it that you have learned from your experience, and send you back to fly again.

It's far, far better to explain to the officials what you *did*, than for them to explain to your survivors what you *should* have done.

The pilot in command is the only judge of his ability to survive in weather conditions he observes ahead of his aircraft. When a non-IFR pilot has been operating in safe weather conditions and subsequently — for whatever reason — finds himself involved in an untenable weather situation, the near-universal solution is a 180 — and a return to known, survivable conditions.

There is nothing so absolutely fundamental to a pilot as survival; and there is no objective that justifies the certain risk of an attempt to continue flight in adverse weather.

Survival is everything.

5 / *Survival Flying Techniques*

Once, while administering a presolo check to a beginning pilot, I noticed all the classic symptoms of a tense person, one with genuine concerns about the outcome of the task at hand. The young lady was a little more voluble than usual, there was just a hint of a tremble in her right hand as she reached for the throttle, and the entire preflight conversation had been punctuated by a nervous little laugh I hadn't noticed before. Once in the air, she was obviously experiencing some difficulty keeping the airplane going the way she intended — the left wing kept dropping, and as soon as she'd bring the wings back to level, the left wing would start down again. In addition to the other signs, she appeared to be hanging on to the control wheel for dear life, and the very weight of her arm was enough to induce a continuous roll to the left.

We straightened out the problem easily enough by changing to a more relaxed grip, and the checkride proceeded more smoothly and proficiently from there on; but this episode points up one of the most common sources of trouble for the non-IFR pilot who finds himself in an instrument situation. Even very small control inputs will cause the airplane to begin excursions from straight-and-level flight, and the scene is set for the various types of disorientation discussed in Chapter 2. As luck (and certain design criteria) would have it, the aircraft axis most sensitive to control pressures is the *roll* axis; a white-knuckled wheel grabber will probably wind up fighting the airplane and, without knowing it, induce the very situation he's trying so hard to avoid.

Introducing "Hands-Off" Flying

Quite literally, most of today's light airplanes will do a *much* better job of flying themselves under normal conditions than an untrained pilot can hope to do. What this chapter will propose (and thoroughly explain) is a *hands-off* method of flying that, in most cases, will provide a greater probability of survival than the inept actions of a pilot who (a) doesn't *know* what to do, and (b) may be in such a state of disorientation that he couldn't make the right moves even if he were properly trained. In order for you to understand what's going on when you put this method to work (you won't believe if you don't understand!), it's necessary to go back to some aerodynamic foundations.

Helping Your Airplane Fly Itself

Nearly all aircraft are designed with a certain amount of stability; that is, when the aircraft is displaced from straight-and-level flight, it tends to return to that condition. Stability was the watchword in the early days of aeronautical design, each inventor coming up with clever ways to keep his machine upright. They reasoned that the unpredictable currents of air would surely upset any airplane that didn't have the power to right itself immediately. Some of the pioneers built flying machines so stable that they couldn't be turned—and a lot of them celebrated first flight and first crash on the same mission, as the unturnable airplane flew into whatever obstacles lay in a straight line from the launch site. Although the Wright brothers' successful vehicle was terribly skittish compared to what you fly today, they achieved success in great measure by arriving at a stability-controllability compromise.

Some airplanes return to straight-and-level flight more readily than others; a lot depends on the intent of the designer. An airline jet transport is very stable because it doesn't need to execute rapid turns or other types of "quick" maneuvers. On the other hand, a fighter or an aerobatic airplane, both of which must dart about the sky if they are to accomplish their respective objectives, are not very stable; control forces are rather light, and they tend to remain in whatever attitude the pilot sets up.

Today's light-airplane fleet, like the Wright Flyer, represents a compromise: a lot of stability in the vertical axis (to control yaw), almost as much in the pitch axis (so that the airplane can be readily trimmed for a particular airspeed), and—this is the important one for IFR survival—*relatively little stability in the roll axis.* If your airplane were designed to be as stable in roll as it is in either yaw or pitch, you wouldn't like the "feel" of the ailerons, and you'd find that banking the airplane for a turn would become hard work.

Your primary flight instructor probably demonstrated yaw stability by gently nudging the nose to left or right, then removing the pedal pressure and showing you that the nose swung back and forth a couple of times, then settled down again straight ahead. It's just as likely that the CFI also showed you how the airplane would gradually level its wings after a gentle bank was induced: considerably slower than the recovery from the yaw displacement, but the airplane did level eventually.

Understanding Hands-Off Flying
And then, the cornerstone of this method of hands-off flying, the demonstration which proved the airplane was stable in pitch. The instructor pulled the nose up well above the horizon, and using rudder pressure to keep the nose on a point, released the control wheel. Almost immediately the nose started down and, perhaps to your concern, kept on going down until it was well *below* the horizon (still no additional inputs from the instructor). The airplane was now racing downhill, engine turning faster, airspeed building; then, like magic, the nose began to ease upward again, through the horizon and up to a point somewhat short of its initial excursion. Down again, though not quite so far, and back up, each oscillation a little less than the one before. Finally, the airplane seemed to have had enough and returned to smooth, steady flight. This was not magic or luck or superengineering; pitch stability is simply the product of a very basic aerodynamic principle.

To begin with, most airplanes are designed so that the center of lift (that infinitely small point through which all the supportive force of the wings is apparently acting) is *behind* the center of gravity (an equally small and imaginary point at which the *weight* of the airplane appears to be concentrated).

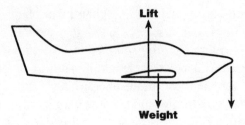

Positioning of the centers of lift and weight results in a nose-down force.

The nose-down force which results is partly offset by thrust—a safety factor of sorts because a *lack* of thrust (as in engine failure) would allow weight to assert itself and pitch the nose downward to maintain flying speed. But thrust can't do the entire job; if it had to, every change in power would cause either a climb or a descent, and you'd have an airplane which would climb and descend at only one airspeed—whatever speed provided the proper relationship of thrust, lift, and weight. Enter the *horizontal stabilizer*, an upside-down airfoil placed at the rear end of the fuselage so that a tail-down force is generated to hold the nose level.

Add an elevator which can vary the downward force at the tail, and the pilot is able to keep the nose where he wants it in terms of pitch attitude. Extra thrust can be translated into more speed; on the other hand, by arresting the nose-down tendency when thrust is reduced, the pilot can fly at a *lower* airspeed.

Left to its own devices, and in consideration of the fact that an airfoil produces more lifting force as airspeed increases, this pitch-control system would ultimately find an airspeed at which the nose-down force (weight) is exactly balanced by the tail-down force (lift) of the horizontal stabilizer.

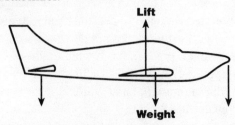

Down-lift generated by the horizontal stabilizer offsets the built-in nose-down force.

Let's say that for some hypothetical airplane this happens at precisely 100 miles per hour, and at that airspeed the pilot decides to demonstrate pitch stability. When he pulls the nose up (no change in power setting, of course), airspeed begins to drop off and with it goes some of the down-lift exerted by the horizontal stabilizer. As soon as the pilot releases the controls, the now nose-heavy plane pitches down and the airspeed builds; as the speed goes beyond 100 miles per hour due to momentum, the nose-up force increases and starts the airplane uphill again. The up-down oscillations will continue, ever decreasing, until the airspeed stabilizes at 100 miles per hour once again—all the forces have been brought into equilibrium.

Airspeed Programming / Straight and Level

The addition of an elevator trim tab provides aerodynamic muscle for the pilot when he wants the airplane to fly at any one of a wide range of airspeeds. When he discovers the angle of attack (directly related to pitch attitude in level flight) and power setting that will maintain altitude at a given airspeed, the trim tab merely "programs" the elevator aerodynamically for that speed; any airspeed greater than that for which it's programmed will make the elevator more effective and cause the nose to pitch up, while any lower airspeed will allow the nose-down tendency to take over.

The response of your airplane to these built-in pitch stability characteristics will vary somewhat from high airspeeds to very low ones; but at normal cruise speed the response will be quite satisfactory, and except for the high-speed airplanes and/or penetration of heavy turbulence, there will be no need to consider changing airspeed until you are near the end of the flight (*see* Chapter 10).

The key to success in the application of this method of hands-off flying is "airspeed programming"—in other words, getting the airplane trimmed so that it will fly reasonably level at normal cruise speed. Unless the whole world begins to come apart at the seams, unless the laws of aerodynamics are repealed while you're up there in the clouds, you should be able to get yourself out of trouble without changing airspeed. Once you've got the elevator programmed for a survivable speed, *leave it that way*. (You should be aware that certain high-wing airplanes tend to change airspeed slightly when power is changed. In any event, the change will be a small one, and in a survival situation it's not enough to be of concern. If your high-winger tends to climb or descend a little faster or slower than the speed for which it was trimmed—programmed—in level flight, not to worry. Whatever results is still a *safe* speed, and that's most important here.)

The Hands-Off Turn

When it comes time to turn (as it must, sooner or later—there are precious few times when salvation lies directly ahead), there's no need to risk overcontrolling by leaning into the ailerons and disturbing the airplane any more than absolutely necessary in its least stable axis. A shallow bank will also take very little vertical lift from the wings, and you'll notice little, if any, deviation in altitude during such a turn. You'll have to watch the artificial horizon to know when you've got what you want, so *very gently* press on the appropriate rudder pedal until the little airplane on the attitude indicator shows a 10-degree bank—no more. Rudder pressure to establish bank angle? You bet. When you cause the airplane to yaw, the outside wing (i.e., the right wing when turning left and vice versa) actually speeds up a bit, therefore developing slightly more lift, and behold—the airplane rolls slowly and positively into a bank, followed by a slow, steady turn.

A 10-degree bank allows the heading change to proceed at a pace that's adequate for the task at hand, and at the same time is slow enough to let you keep up with what's happening. When it's time to roll out of the turn, apply just enough pressure to the rudder pedal to bring the little airplane back to level flight, and keep it that way. The secret is small, consistent amounts of rudder *pressure*—just enough to get the job done. There's some skill involved here, and you *must* practice this technique before you need to use it.

The Hands-Off Descent

So much for level flight. At some point in the process of getting out of this predicament, you must descend. There's a built-in trap for the untrained pilot who pushes the nose over in order to go down; the inevitable result is increased airspeed, which is something you don't need right now. Rather, consider this: in its level-flight, airspeed-programmed condition, your airplane requires a certain amount of thrust to maintain altitude. The pitch attitude is responsible for the control of airspeed (remember the pitch stability demonstration on Page 47), so it follows that power—engine output translated into thrust by the propeller—is maintaining the altitude you've selected.

If the power setting is changed, something's got to give (assuming that you are flying hands-off), and it will be altitude. Following a power reduction, however slight, there will be an almost imperceptible decrease in airspeed, unnoticed except by the horizontal stabilizer, which is very sensitive to airflow changes. Even a slight change in speed results in less *down*-load on the tail, whereupon the designed-in nose heaviness exerts its influence, and the airplane will pitch down ever so slightly to maintain the airspeed for which you have it trimmed. When this happens, the airplane will commence descending at a rate directly proportional to the amount of thrust you have removed.

Easy Does It

This is new country you're exploring, so move slowly. If yours is a fixed-pitch propeller installation, take a deep breath, place your right hand on the throttle, and *squeeze* it outward until the tachometer shows a reduction of 100 rpm—no more! With a controllable-pitch propeller, your initial power change should be not more than 1 inch of manifold pressure. When everything is squared away and you see that you are indeed moving away from the original altitude at a very slow rate, decrease power another 100 rpm (1 inch), followed by similar incremental reductions until a satisfactory rate of descent is established. Take small steps, and you'll not overcontrol.

In any event, no matter how badly you want to get out of the clouds, don't let your anxiety for lower altitudes lead you down the garden path; the maximum rate of descent in a survival situation should be 500 feet per minute. In most light airplanes, this rate is accomplished when the power has been reduced by approximately 500 rpm or 5 inches of manifold pressure.

The best possible outcome would see you descending slowly and steadily until you break out of the clouds, from whence you can continue in everyday VFR conditions. Should you be required to level off while still cloud-bound, it's a simple matter of replacing the thrust you took away. Again, *squeeze* the throttle until the airplane has stopped descending; the tachometer or manifold pressure gauge should be very close to its original level-flight indication.

Hands-Off Heading Control

One of the greatest features of flying turbojet airplanes is the complete absence of the directional-control problems caused by a propeller when power is changed; remember "P factor" from your study of basic aerodynamics? When there's a propeller or two pulling your airplane through the air, you can't get away with feet-on-the-floor flying like your jet-powered brethren; you must apply whatever rudder pressure is necessary to keep the nose from swinging to left or right as you change power. A simple rule will help you anticipate this problem and lick it before it starts: whenever (at a constant airspeed) power is reduced, the nose will yaw to the right—you'll need to apply *left* rudder pressure to maintain the heading; the opposite is true when power is increased. And be advised that you'll have to hold that rudder pressure (or trim it off if your airplane is so equipped) until power is once again at the level-flight setting. Now that you know what will happen, anticipate the effect and make the heading indicator stay put with whatever rudder inputs are required.

The Hands-Off Climb

VFR pilots who become embroiled in battles with IFR conditions will probably commence their adventures at a safe altitude, safe at least with regard to obstacle clearance, and the "save" usually employs a descent to VFR conditions. On that rare occasion when you might need to increase altitude in order to achieve visual flight conditions or climb over an intervening obstacle, you should be aware of the technique that will see you safely to a higher altitude. Starting from a normal, airspeed-programmed cruise condition, climbing is very much the opposite of the descent just discussed; you need only add enough power to climb at the desired rate—which, just like the descent, doesn't need to be a screamer. The objective is to increase altitude just enough to be safe, and you're in no hurry.

When climb time comes, *squeeze* the throttle slowly until you see an rpm increase of 100 (or an additional 1 inch of manifold pressure). The heading indicator will creep to the left, and you'll stop that with the appropriate amount of right rudder pressure. Now add another 100 rpm (1 inch of manifold pressure), monitor the heading indicator to determine how much more rudder pressure is required, and so on until you have increased power by 500 rpm (5 inches of manifold pressure) or full throttle, whichever comes first. When the desired altitude is achieved, reduce the power setting (*squeeze!*) until the airplane stops climbing. The power numbers should be very close to what they were down lower. Make small corrections (on the order of 50–100 rpm or ½–1 inch) if the airplane tends to climb or descend after level-off; keep the altimeter within a couple hundred feet of the target, and you're doing fine.

So much for the aerodynamic considerations and control inputs to achieve safe flight in the clouds; however, no flying technique can be successful unless you know how to determine when your objectives have been met. In other words, which of the instruments should you watch to know when your control inputs are doing the job? Right off the bat, you must understand that without the specialized training and practice that develop true instrument-flying skills, *you cannot successfully interpret all of the information before you.* You need a bare-bones instrument scan.

Proceeding on the assumption that you got into the clouds in a normal cruise condition, and that the airplane was trimmed for level flight, the flight instruments which become *absolutely necessary* for aircraft control are reduced to only two—the attitude indicator and the heading indicator. Rivet your attention on these two, with infrequent glances at the others for confirmation, and you'll do a much better job than the pilot who tries—despite lack of training in instrument scan and cross-check, two cornerstones of *real* IFR operations— to cover everything at the same time. Don't attempt it, because it can't be done reliably without proper training.

During those portions of your survival flight that are of the straight-and-level variety (with any kind of luck, that should be most of the time), close attention to heading and attitude will detect the very beginnings of those small but persistent changes that are bound to occur. You must expect slight excursions in heading, but the importance of detection and correction while the excursions are small cannot be emphasized enough. Be careful not to fall into the yo-yo mode, wherein rudder pressure is being constantly applied first to one side, then the other; it's likely that you'll need to hold some constant pressure to keep the numbers where you want them.

Level flight can be easily maintained within ±200 feet or so of the desired altitude by an occasional check of the altimeter and an accompanying *small* adjustment in power setting if necessary (*small* means no more than 50–100 rpm, or ½–1 inch of manifold pressure). Don't retrim the elevator; that will only change the programmed airspeed, and when you've got a good thing going (acceptable airspeed) don't jump out of the frying pan.

When a turn is required, forget the heading indicator momentarily and focus on the attitude indicator. *Squeeze* on the appropriate rudder pedal until you see the bank angle beginning to change, and maintain that pressure until the little airplane's wingtip indicates a 10-degree bank. Ease off on the rudder pressure just enough to maintain the 10-degree wing-down attitude, then glance at the heading indicator to see how you're doing. As the desired heading number approaches the top of the instrument, *squeeze* some pressure on the rollout rudder pedal until the airplane is once again upright. Don't try to roll out right on the number; if you have to make a small post-rollout correction, that's okay. Whatever you do, don't allow the bank to exceed 10 degrees, and be satisfied if you can stop the turn within 10 or 15 degrees of the desired heading. This is *not* an accuracy drill.

In like manner, you must pay close attention to the heading indicator when entering a climb or descent, or leveling off from either of those maneuvers. The culprit is the yaw induced by propeller forces as power is changed, and your need to heed the reading of the heading indicator is more important than anything else at this point. The suggestion that you accomplish all power changes in very small increments for climbs, descents, and level-offs was not made lightly; by limiting your power changes to no more than 100 rpm (1 inch of manifold pressure) at a time, you'll never bite off more yaw than you can chew. There's no hurry.

Head in a Vise

Yet another good reason for limiting your instrument scan primarily to two indicators has to do with the physiological problems discussed in Chapter 2. Close your eyes for a moment and imagine the instrument panel of the airplane you fly most frequently, the one in which you are most likely to need this technique; if your head is pointing directly at the center of the panel in front of you, there's probably nothing else on that panel—even the gauges on the far side—that you can't see without turning your head, right? Most of our lightplanes have only engine gauges and radios over there anyway, and there's very infrequent need to refer to them in a survival situation.

Even slight head movements may induce spatial disorientation, the very condition you are most interested in preventing. Resist the temptation to look around the cockpit; if you must check something else on the panel, move only your eyes. You can pick up the microphone and talk, put your hand on a frequency knob, do almost anything that's necessary for continued flight without moving your head. You may even develop an ache from holding the old brainbox in one position for a long time, but better a sore neck than a busted one. In those situations which absolutely require head movement, do so ver-r-r-y slowly, and *never* while the airplane is turning. During a turn, you must place the greatest emphasis on strict attention to the attitude indicator, and nothing else; this is the time when your vertigo vulnerability is the greatest.

"George" Means Well, But...

If, when you find yourself in Survival City, you happen to be flying an airplane equipped with a wing leveler or a full-fledged autopilot, you're way ahead of the problem—assuming, of course, that you know how to engage and operate that appliance. Every contemporary autopilot system incorporates a wing leveler, which eliminates the danger of entering the dread high-speed spiral dive. There are so many different types of autopilots that only two operational generalities can be offered: first, don't use the autopilot unless you know how (or are provided adequate instruction over the radio from someone who really knows the system), and second, do not use the VOR tracking mode in a survival situation. The tracking function causes the airplane to turn until it intercepts whatever radial is selected on the VOR indicator, then follow it to the station. While it seems an outstanding pilot aid at first, the tracking mode generates heading changes without being commanded by the pilot, and therefore without his knowledge — threshold of rotation and all that, and the disorientation problems that go with it.

Of particular concern is the situation which results when the autopilot's tracking mode has brought the airplane right over the VOR transmitter. You know from experience that the VOR course needle gets very unsteady close-in, and the autopilot will do its best to follow that nervous needle. In addition to a series of turns in both directions as the needle moves back and forth, the autopilot will usually produce a large heading change as it attempts to reintercept the course on the other side of the station. All of this maneuvering is just about guaranteed to make your head swim.

Altitude changes with the help of an autopilot are a piece of cake, since the yawing movements induced by a power change will never be noticed. No matter, you must still squeeze the throttle and observe the small incremental changes discussed earlier. Give "George" a break, too.

In summary then, the hands-off technique for surviving in an IFR situation:

- Have the airplane trimmed for normal, level-flight cruise before you get into trouble (which means that you should fly this way all the time).

- Focus your attention on the attitude indicator and the heading indicator, and resolve to keep your head movements to an absolute minimum until you're once again in visual conditions.

- Take your hands off the wheel and use judicious rudder pressure to control heading, trusting to the speed-programmed elevator for pitch control.

- Make very small adjustments in power if necessary to maintain the desired altitude within ±200 feet, and whenever you change the throttle setting, *squeeze*.

- For turns, lock your eyes onto the attitude indicator and press the appropriate rudder pedal until the airplane shows a 10-degree bank, followed by just enough rudder pressure to maintain that attitude. When the heading indicator shows that you're approaching the desired direction, *press* gently on the opposite rudder until the airplane is upright again. Make very small corrections after the turn if necessary; be happy if you're within ±10 – 15 degrees of what you want.

- To descend, reduce power 100 rpm or 1 inch of manifold pressure to get things started, rudder pressure as required to keep the heading glued on the proper number. When you feel comfortable with the initial rate of descent, reduce power by another small increment, stabilize again, and continue this process until you have *squeezed* off no more than 500 rpm or 5 inches of manifold pressure.

- Level off from a descent by gradually increasing power (in the same small increments) until the airplane has stopped descending, indicated by the altimeter hands coming to a halt. Make small power adjustments as necessary to maintain the new altitude.

- Should a climb be required, increase power in increments of 100 rpm or 1 inch of manifold pressure until you have added 500 rpm (5 inches) or full throttle, whichever happens first. Level off by reducing power until the airplane is able to stay at the new altitude, then make minor throttle adjustments as required.

- If you have an autopilot, use it only if you know how, and stay away from the tracking mode. Make the autopilot fly the headings that *you* command.

What Could Possibly Go Wrong?

Realizing that strong yaw stability is designed into the airplane, and that you will program the elevator for cruise airspeed so that pitch stability is taken care of, return for a moment to the real troublemaker, roll stability — or lack thereof. Most of today's lightplanes will recover quite handily if they are placed in, say, a 20-degree bank in either direction and then left to their own devices. The recovery to level flight will likely be a little on the slow side, but the subtle forces at work will eventually bring things back to normal. However, there's an angle of bank beyond which your airplane will *not* recover; the airplane will roll into an even steeper bank, lower its nose, and head for the ground in a hurry.

Please, Lord, *Not* a Spiral Dive

If corrective action is not taken in this situation, the aerodynamic forces combine to set up a spiral dive in which nose attitude continues downward, airspeed continues to build (usually at an alarming rate), and the angle of bank gets steeper and steeper. Most unfortunately, the untrained pilot may not even notice the slight turn which got this whole thing started—remember the threshold of rotation (Pages 16–17), below which the sensing mechanisms of your inner ear cannot tell a turn has begun?—and by the time you realize what has happened, airspeed, bank angle, turn rate, pitch attitude, and the accompanying centrifugal force have built up to potentially disastrous levels.

In some cases, airplanes come apart solely by virtue of the excessive airspeeds generated in a near-vertical dive at cruise power. But the most common finale of this disoriented performance comes when the pilot realizes that something life-threatening is taking place, and he applies the one type of control response that he deems most effective in this situation—a healthy pull on the control column. With the airplane wrapped up in a steep bank and the nose pointed nearly straight down, any up-elevator force may be enough to overstress the tail surfaces, and shortly after the tail departs the airplane, it begins to shed other appurtenances, such as wings, engines, windshields, and the like.

The best solution to the spiral dive problem is, of course, prevention—don't let yourself get there in the first place. That's an unrealistic approach to your survival, because it can happen. You'll know, oh how you'll know! The heading indicator will be literally spinning, the airspeed indicator will be moving rapidly toward the red line, altimeter unwinding like you've never seen it unwind before, turn indicator at full deflection on one side or the other. But the most unusual and frightening warnings will be those you feel and hear; you're pressed down in your seat by centrifugal force, the air noise will be at a level you've never experienced before, and the engine will be making sounds that are totally foreign to normal operations—especially if you're flying behind a fixed-pitch propeller, which speeds up in proportion to airspeed.

The Recovery — or Giving it Your Best Shot

The remedy is simple in principle, but may well turn out to be the most difficult task you've ever performed, to say nothing of its importance! If you don't do something soon, the airplane is surely going to tear itself apart, and with speed one of the worst villains, the first thing to do is reduce power, quickly and completely. No time for the careful squeezing that's been advocated up to this point; you must slow the airplane now.

With throttle closed, your next job is to level the wings, and, at the high airspeeds that may prevail, it will take a lot more force than you've had to use on the wheel before. But roll you must, and the turn indicator (left-right needle, or the little airplane symbol if yours is a "turn coordinator") becomes the primary instrument to determine which way to roll. It's likely that the attitude indicator has tumbled because of the extreme bank angle, and it is subject to gross misinterpretation in this situation; go with the turn indicator. If it's displaced to the left, apply aileron to the right, and vice versa. *The turn indicator will always tell you the truth about which direction the airplane is turning, even if you're inverted.*

Now comes the touchy part—stopping the descent. You must treat this part of the recovery procedure with kid gloves, because of the possibility of overstressing the tail. Begin pressing the control column backward to raise the nose, using the seat of your pants as the indicator for "how much." You need to maintain a "heavy" feeling in order to get the job done, but when that sensation begins to get very uncomfortable, ease off a bit. Keep the airplane going straight (turn indicator again; the heading indicator may have also tumbled) and continue your slow, steady pull on the wheel until the altimeter stops unwinding. You're once again in level flight when the altimeter stops, but of course power is at idle; so you must adjust the throttle to what you know should be a normal cruise setting, and start all over again.

Let's be very candid about recovery from a well-developed spiral dive: the chances of success for an untrained VFR-only pilot are quite small. But since the alternative is so unacceptable, you might as well give it your best shot. If you've never been in a situation like this, get an instructor to demonstrate a couple of spirals and recoveries. Seems like pretty good life insurance.

Stall/Spin Recovery

A spin is very much the same as a spiral dive, with airspeed the major difference. Where the speed in a spiral dive is very high and increasing, a spin will take place at a very *low* airspeed, with little or no change as the maneuver progresses. You'll feel some of the centrifugal forces in a spin, but there will not be the wild rush of air, nor will the engine be screaming.

Recovery is also similar, with the exception that you must get the airplane out of the turn with rudder, not aileron (use of aileron during a spin will usually aggravate the condition). The turn indicator once again comes to the fore as the primary helper in deciding which rudder to push, and of course you must reduce power to idle just as soon as you determine that something has gone wrong. The same gentle pull on the control wheel will stop the dive that results as soon as the turn is stopped, and from there on the recovery procedure is identical to that used for a spiral dive. A spin is much less likely to occur in an IFR survival situation, because you must slow the airplane, stall it, and maintain the stalled condition for a spin to occur and continue.

An inadvertent stall (even an inadvertent *approach* to a stall, in which airspeed is falling off rapidly for whatever reason) must be countered quickly and positively, because of the possibility of the airplane falling off into a spin or a spiral dive. If all the indicators tell you that a stall is about to happen — airspeed low and continuing to decrease, the rush of air around the cabin getting quieter and quieter, engine slowing down, nose high, stall warner sounding the alarm — you must act right away. Go to *full power*, apply whatever elevator pressure is required to make the altimeter hands stand still, level the wings on the attitude indicator, and when flight conditions approach normal again, revert to your previous power settings and control inputs … and don't let *that* happen again!

When Hands-Off Needs a Hand

Turbulent air creates even more problems for a VFR pilot involved in a survival operation. All the aerodynamic principles discussed so far will work, but your technique must change when the air gets lumpy... you've got to work harder, that's for sure. Hands-off will probably not do the job because of the excursions from normal flight attitudes as a result of the turbulence; you will have to put your hands on the wheel and help the airplane fly itself. The pilot's task in turbulence is not so much that of actually flying the airplane; it's more of a *damping* influence—watching for the big excursions in pitch and bank, and applying control pressure to bring things back to normal. Your ride will be rough, and grossly uncoordinated at times, but concentrate on the attitude indicator and keep the wings and pitch attitude as nearly level as you can. Rough, gross control inputs are not necessary or desirable here; just enough of you on the controls to keep the airplane's movements within reasonable limits. Again, there's nothing like a training session under the hood on a turbulent day to condition you for the real thing if it ever happens.

Author's Introduction to Chapter 6

I believe in consulting specialists — and that's why, when I have an earache, I don't go to a foot doctor. Using that philosophy, I recognized that one of the most difficult parts of IFR survival flying is conquering the problems of the human element involved. Jerry Cockrell is a flight instructor, a veteran lecturer in CFI revalidation programs, and most important for our purposes here, a psychologist who has specialized in the problems of pilots under stress. So that you would have the advantage of the best possible information about what to expect from yourself in a survival situation, and to help convince you that you *can* fly yourself out of trouble, I asked Dr. Cockrell to set down his thoughts on the subject.

—R.L.T.

The pilot in command is the only judge of his ability to survive in weather conditions he observes ahead of his aircraft. When a non-IFR pilot has been operating in safe weather conditions and subsequently—for whatever reason—finds himself involved in an untenable weather situation, the near-universal solution is a 180—and a return to known, survivable conditions.

There is nothing so absolutely fundamental to a pilot as survival; and there is no objective that justifies the certain risk of an attempt to continue flight in adverse weather.

Survival is everything.

6 / The Human Element in IFR Survival

by Dr. Jerald D. Cockrell

After reading about the specific steps to take in order to manipulate an aircraft safely in a low-visibility environment, you may be thinking, "Yeah, those ideas make a lot of sense. But I wonder if I could actually do all those things if the pressure were really on?"

From flying lesson number one, all aviators are concerned about their own ability to handle emergencies. We hear of pilots who have encountered a wide variety of harrowing situations, and usually these stories only lead to more self-doubt in the minds of the listeners. Regarding self-concepts, most flight instructors are careful not to allow their students to become overconfident, lest they develop flaws in judgment that will lead them into flight situations beyond their actual capabilities. Nevertheless, it is also the instructor's responsibility to develop a student's self-esteem to the point that he or she can function effectively in unusual circumstances.

You're beginning to catch on now, right? The *human* element, or "I can learn lots of neat techniques and procedures, but will I be able to implement them if the need arises?" Yes, you certainly *can*! It's been done by others, and it will be done again. You *can* develop the human capabilities to handle stressful situations in a very positive manner.

Humans react differently to stress. You've heard a cool, calm pilot described as one who "has ice water flowing through his veins." Well, maybe so, and maybe not. Training and experience play an important part in this *apparent* lack of concern, but the trained, experienced pilot still has a human reaction to stressful events—the difference is that he has learned how to channel *thoughts* into positive, productive efforts. In other words, don't dwell on how bad things *are* or what terrible things *could* happen; instead, use that energy to concentrate on the best ways to solve this problem in a positive way.

Professional golfers are experts in concentration, since a major portion of the game is mental. So what do you suppose those folks are thinking about during a tournament—that last shot that hooked out of bounds? No way. They're concentrating on here and now, and how good the *next* shot is going to be. We have to discipline ourselves to think positively in tough situations and get busy doing something to help ourselves. More on the action items later.

How We Behave Under Stress

In a suddenly stressful situation that carries the possibility of disaster, many people go through a very definite and time-consuming sequence of reactions. These behavioral phases have been verified by people who have gone through some really trying times, such as aviation emergencies. Perhaps, if you know ahead of time what to expect from yourself, you'll be better equipped to analyze an emergency situation and cope with it successfully.

The first phase is *denial*. This is where you try to mentally extricate yourself from a potentially hazardous environment. It's the old "this can't be happening to me" routine. Some people *never* get past this conflict with reality and they are probably still arguing with themselves about it when they hit the ground. If you are somehow able to face the reality of the moment, you will likely begin to work furiously at recalling procedures, going through checklists, and trying out all sorts of things in order to remedy the problem. After going over and over and over these procedures you may, in effect, reach the end of your computer tape. "I've run out of things to do—can't think of anything else that might work."

At this point you might go into a phase that I have termed the *confusion/inactivity* phase, which is pilot talk for "I have just become a passenger." You might be able to break out of this unproductive, do-nothing state by telling yourself—*aloud*—to get busy and *do* something. Tell yourself that you *will* succeed, and keep saying it.

Usually, just after breaking out of the confusion/inactivity phase, most people report a feeling of *anger*. Anger at the airplane, at the system, at your passengers (for talking you into this), and anger at yourself (for letting them do it).

The anger tends to subside rather quickly, to be replaced by *challenge*. "Okay, if this is it, I'll make the best of it. My best chance to survive is to be in charge, control the aircraft and myself, and to do what I've been taught." Now you're getting somewhere.

Let's take another look at this progression of human reactions to stress. Although it's tough to face, the sooner you get into reality, the more time you'll have to spend on survival procedures. Confusion/inactivity comes when you give up. Keep on trying, concentrate, try some more. Anger is another normal but time-consuming and out-of-control segment. Save it until later and move on to the challenge phase, where you'll be rewarded for bringing forth all your real flying talents.

Recognize the Signs

Physically, there are many signs that stress is at work. Again, they vary from person to person, but there are some easily identified symptoms: sweaty palms (that's just about standard), rapid or increased breathing rate, tight grip on the controls, pounding in the head or ears, tight neck, tight abdominal muscles, shaky hands or knees, quivering voice, and so on. You may even realize that you've experienced all of those—and at the same time!

Often the realization that we are beginning to tighten up makes us even *more* uptight. What you and I must do, beginning right now, is to let these signs of stress work *for* us instead of against us. Many people try unsuccessfully to get control of these symptoms. Usually, the failure to gain control is because we are merely trying to *cover* those weaknesses. "Weaknesses? Not me—that would mean that I am less than perfect and that I am fallible." Let's go right to the net. The fact is that we are *all* fallible, and we do make mistakes and have some weaknesses, and so what? So my hands shake and my voice quavers; that doesn't make me any less of a person. See what's happening? We need to be using all that energy to do something productive.

Take Action

Instead of suppressing these symptoms, I suggest another way to deal with them. It's the ERP method, in which E stands for *express*, R for *replace*, and P for *prevent*.

Expressing symptoms rather than fighting and trying to suppress them is quite helpful. If your hands are trembling, shake them even more violently—exaggerate it! Seems kinda funny, doesn't it? Good. Laugh *aloud* at yourself. It works wonders. Are your palms sweaty? Try making them sweat a little more (good luck). If your voice is quavering, make yourself yodel (please don't key the microphone at this point). "I just feel like screaming!" So, yell out loud. (You must realize, of course, that once you're safely back on the ground, your flying partners will probably throw the cargo net over you and try to cart you off to the Happy Hotel, but right now, who cares.) Remember when you were a kid and had to walk past the cemetery or through some other scary place alone? Remember how *whistling* seemed to make you feel all better? The same principle applies here, although to tell the truth, I have always had a tough time whistling while running at top speed. In the airplane it's not a question of fight or flight—it's fight *and* flight. And it can be done.

One more point on the express technique. Most pilots talk aloud to themselves when flying solo, and this fits right in with our program. Try to imagine your old flight instructor sitting right beside you and watching everything you do. This should help boost your confidence, because most of us, when talking to ourselves, are saying what our instructors would say. Remember that first solo? You always *thought* your instructor was totally cool and calm, but we instructors are human too; on a CFI checkride, we have to demonstrate that we can sweat only on the right sides of our faces!

Replace is next. Research has shown and common sense will agree that it is a practical impossibility to be both anxious and relaxed at the same time. One inhibits the other. The key here is to develop your own skill at relaxing and to call upon this skill whenever a normally anxiety-producing situation is encountered.

Learn to Relax

Relaxation skills may be learned through several methods. Training in progressive relaxation (my personal favorite), biofeedback, meditation, self-hypnosis, etc., is readily available. Books, audiotapes, and personal training seminars are abundant. These skills require practice, but most folks can quickly learn the techniques and can use them at will. There are some similarities in the various methods, and one of these is deep breathing. While deep breathing may be a complete study in itself, its basic concepts are relevant to a stressful inflight situation. I have found that taking just three deep breaths can do a world of good in a tough spot. Breathe in deeply, hold the breath for about three seconds and then let the breath completely out. You'll be pleasantly surprised at how effective this can be even when you're very tense.

Most muscle-relaxation techniques incorporate eye-closing as part of the training routine. This is done simply to allow the participant to concentrate on his own body and not on the surrounding environment. After learning how to relax effectively, you will find that the eye-closing part is not always required; in fact, I wouldn't really recommend *that* part for the flying situation. So, instead of being tense you *can* be relaxed. Remember, you can't do both at the same time.

Although *prevention* is listed last, it really should be first. Why do you suppose professional pilots are able to handle most emergencies in a relatively calm and orderly fashion? The fact is, they get that way through training and experience. Even though most of those folks really don't care much for the hours and hours of simulator training that they are required to endure, when the going gets tough the training comes through. The *team* begins to work. Everyone has a job. It's all pretty well coordinated.

Practice Makes Ready

But what about the single-pilot type of operation? And what if you're not able to obtain extensive cockpit- and emergency-procedures training? Then you'll have to devise a special approach to the problem. As we all no doubt agree, in-depth knowledge usually overcomes fear. And while this first step is not a new one, it is a neglected and seldom practiced one and it *is* knowledge related — I'm referring to the blindfold cockpit check. Many of us were required to be thoroughly proficient in this test of knowledge, but the procedure seems to have been dropped from most training programs. In the clouds, by yourself, in turbulence, at night, is not the time to fumble for light switches, radio controls, and other important cockpit features. Lack of familiarity here just creates another anxiety-producing element. Go sit in the airplane you usually fly, and challenge yourself to a thorough checkout of all the important items and locations; do this on a regular basis. The payoff comes when you get into a tight spot and need to be concentrating on other things.

It's been said many times, but it's well worth another mention: thorough preflight planning, knowledge of weather situations, and possible alternatives are vital to safe flight. At this point, don't let your ego get in the way of making a no go decision. You know what they say — "It's better to be down here wishing you were up there than to be up there wishing you were down here!"

Prevention certainly extends to actual inflight practice. As mentioned in the previous chapter, practicing the suggested techniques is absolutely essential. It's a great confidence booster as well. I cannot overemphasize the value of trying out survival flying procedures *before* getting into an emergency situation. Remember the pro pilot: practice, experience, and more practice. After you're in the clouds is a poor time to begin experimenting with unfamiliar survival techniques.

One more shot of preparation. Although it may seem like a difficult thing to do, you *can* prepare yourself to maintain control both mentally and physically. You must discipline yourself to *think ahead*. Even before going out to the airport, you should question yourself about this flight. It's a lot like a chess game — what would I do if this or that happened? Just at rotation is *not* the time for a multi-engine pilot to begin reviewing engine-out procedures. Try to anticipate every possibility. You may not cover everything, but you'll leave a lot fewer loose ends.

Let's review what you've learned about the human aspects of handling inflight stress:

- Recognize the phases of human behavior under stress (*denial, confusion/inactivity, anger, challenge*), and try to jump ahead to the challenge phase.

- Recognize physical signs of stress and begin to counteract these reactions by putting them to use (express, replace, prevent—the ERP method).
- Take three deep breaths.
- *Express* yourself and then move on.
- *Replace* stress symptoms with trained-in relaxation procedures.
- *Prevent* such a heavy stress load through training, practice, and anticipation.

The pilot in command is the only judge of his ability to survive in weather conditions he observes ahead of his aircraft. When a non-IFR pilot has been operating in safe weather conditions and subsequently — for whatever reason — finds himself involved in an untenable weather situation, the near-universal solution is a 180 — and a return to known, survivable conditions.

There is nothing so absolutely fundamental to a pilot as survival; and there is no objective that justifies the certain risk of an attempt to continue flight in adverse weather.

Survival is everything.

7 / *Radar*

Way back in 1863, a prominent scientist, James Clerk Maxwell, figured out that radio waves and light waves behaved very much alike; he reasoned that if light were reflected from mirrors, radio waves would probably be reflected from metallic surfaces. He was right, of course, and so the theoretical foundation of radar was laid. Radar—an acronym for **ra**dio **d**etection **a**nd **r**anging—has become *the* primary tool of Air Traffic Control in this country; without it, our air transportation system would no doubt collapse overnight. Radar pervades our airspace; it's difficult to imagine a pilot learning to fly without being exposed to it, and even more unlikely that an aviator could have flown for very long in the United States without taking advantage of its benefits.

But radar is not the ultimate crutch for a pilot, because it has limitations and restrictions. The VFR pilot who depends totally on radar in any predicament may be in for an unpleasant surprise if he happens to get into trouble in an area where radar can't help. Some understanding is in order.

Basic radar utilizes the reflective nature of metallic objects to return a portion of a radio beam to the antenna from which it was fired. A computer figures out how much time was required for the signal to make the round trip, and from that information it can determine the distance between antenna and object. (A good low-speed analogy would have you holler down a canyon, note the time until the echo comes back, then figure out the distance to the far wall by virtue of your knowledge of the speed of sound.) At the same time, the electronic brain is able to figure out the azimuth, or angular displacement of the object relative to the antenna, and a positive location results. When the signals are processed and displayed on a cathode-ray tube (the radar-scope), the controllers have a rather accurate display of the where-abouts of certain aircraft within the operating range of the equipment.

Enter the Transponder

Unfortunately, things other than airplanes reflect radio energy — raindrops and mountaintops, for example. To keep the scopes from becoming cluttered with meaningless returns, and to provide the con-trollers with very positive indications with which to go about their business of traffic separation, computer-generated radar images were phased into the system, and black boxes called radar transponders were introduced. Also known as radar beacons, transponders return a *coded* signal to the radar site, where it is processed and displayed on the screen. By assigning a discrete code to each aircraft so equipped, the controllers can track its progress through the airspace with a great deal more accuracy and definition. When you are assigned a specific tran-sponder code, yours is the only aircraft in the immediate area using that code — and your return can be readily and positively identified.

Standard "Squawks"

Each instrument flight is assigned a transponder code before takeoff, and, barring unusual happenings within the computer system, that code will not be changed throughout the flight. It's an electronic tag which the IFR flight carries all the way to destination — even if it's clear across the country. There is also a series of standard codes, to be used in specific airborne situations: 1200 for all VFR flights not assigned a discrete code, 7700 to draw ATC's attention to an emergency, 7600 for an aircraft which has suffered loss of communications capability, and 7500, which is reserved for use by a pilot whose aircraft is being "un-lawfully interfered with" — in other words, hijacked.

Two of these standard codes are of particular interest for this discussion of survival in IFR conditions: the VFR squawk, 1200, and the international emergency code, 7700. (Transponder codes are called squawks, and the term becomes a verb in aeronautical lingo. When the transponder was introduced as a very positive aerial identification system during World War II — the original descriptor was IFF [identification, friend or foe] — it didn't take long for military pilots to come up with a clever code word for the new black boxes on their aircraft. Since the transponder "repeats" what it "hears," they tagged it "parrot," and of course parrots "squawk," and the verbiage has stuck to this day.)

Contemporary radar displays do not always show VFR flights — that is, those squawking 1200 — because the screen must be kept uncluttered so that controllers will have a clearer field for their first-priority business, looking after IFR traffic. But the 1200 signal is "seen" and remembered by the computer, ready for instant display if necessary.

When a pilot squawks 7700, every radar set that has acquired that signal will display a very distinctive flashing word, EMRG, near the aircraft's position on the screen — *that* should get someone's attention!

A Squawk in Time...

There are two points to be made here: first, *always* squawk 1200 when you're flying VFR (unless, of course, you're in contact with a controller who has assigned a discrete code for traffic advisories); second, whenever you find yourself in a situation that calls for immediate alerting of a ground radar facility and you haven't been able to establish radio communications, squawk 7700. It's possible, in certain parts of the country and at certain altitudes, to be outside the range of ATC radar, but when you need help, pull out all the stops. It's probably best to listen on 121.5 in this case; somebody will more than likely be trying to contact you.

Most of today's light-airplane transponders have five functions: OFF, STANDBY (in this mode the set is powered but is not replying to any signals from the ground and is therefore returning no signals), ON (or in some cases, NORMAL), ALT (for altitude reporting capability), and TEST, which, when selected, turns on a green light to show that all is well within the set. This light will also probably glow every time the transponder is interrogated by a ground station. Some units incorporate the ability to take an electronic look at the altimeter and send that information back to the ground radar; there it is processed and displayed on the controller's screen in feet above mean sea level.

You may on occasion be asked to "squawk ident": press the appropriately labeled button on the transponder, and your display on the radar screen will be reinforced for about thirty seconds for positive identification. The ident function is a great feature of the transponder, especially when the controller is trying to pick you out of the crowd on his scope.

The Radar Assist

Radio communications during a radar-guided rescue are very simple: Acknowledge the headings and altitudes provided by the controller, answer his questions as they come up, and *fly the airplane*. You should expect to be handled by only one person, since the supervisor will normally assign the first controller you contact to continue until you're out of trouble or out of that controller's area of responsibility, whichever happens first. If you *are* required to change frequencies along the way (an unlikely circumstance unless it's a long, long way to VFR conditions), make a note of the current frequency before you change the numbers on the radio. If you can't establish communications on the new frequency, it's mighty nice to have the old one handy. Jot the numbers on your note pad, on your trouser leg, on the back of your hand, or on the frequency selector of the number two radio. If all else fails, go to 121.5 and holler—someone will hear you.

Since inclement weather is at the heart of everything in this book, there is a radar limitation of which you should be acutely aware; today's radar, as utilized by the Air Route Traffic Control Centers, is designed to display en route traffic very clearly, and one of the features lost in the compromise is *weather* information—specifically, the location of precipitation. When you are struggling through the clouds, using every bit of your severely limited IFR skills just to remain upright and headed in the proper direction, the last thing you need is an encounter with heavy rain and the turbulence that usually goes with it. Controllers will check other sources to obtain information regarding areas of precipitation, but you must not assume that you're home free just because the controller says there is no weather on the scope.

Flying a Radar Approach

Sooner or later during an exercise in survival (please, Lord, let it be *sooner!*), you're going to arrive in a terminal area and be faced with the problem of flying your airplane to a point from which you can make visual contact with the ground or a runway and land safely. When you have been shepherded through the cloudy skies by an en route radar controller, you're well set up to finish the job, because a radar approach merely continues the series of vectors (headings supplied by the controller) to align your aircraft with the landing runway and put you within sight of Mother Earth. The only airborne equipment required for a radar approach is a functioning radio transmitter and receiver, and you can even get along without a transmitter; if you can hear the controller's instructions, you can fly out of trouble.

As a general rule, airports with radar facilities (Approach Control) can provide the navigational guidance and low-workload procedure you need. A radar approach demands no more of a pilot than following instructions—mostly headings, occasional altitude changes—and looking for the runway at the appropriate time. In almost every case the controller will be using a published procedure, one that has been established in advance for the use of instrument pilots.

There are two distinct types of radar approaches—precision and surveillance—but the former has found so little use in our air traffic system that it is all but nonexistent. Most Air Force and Navy air installations maintain their own precision radar approach units; they incorporate three-dimensional guidance, with a glideslope in addition to azimuth and range, and they can guide an airplane right down to the runway in zero-zero conditions if necessary. It's hardly a routine operation, but if your emergency happens when all the civilian airports around are really "socked in" and there's an Air Force or Navy base handy with an operating precision radar system, they'll guide you to a landing. You can take care of the paperwork and explain your unauthorized use of a military installation after you're safely on the ground!

Surveillance Approach Procedure

Given the proliferation of radar-equipped civilian airports, the most likely candidate for your salvation will be a surveillance procedure. You'll be furnished headings to fly to align the aircraft with the extended centerline of the landing runway. The controller will, if necessary, ease you down to an appropriate altitude to begin the approach, and at a predetermined distance from the runway advise you to begin descent to a specific minimum altitude. In IFR parlance, this is known as the MDA, or minimum descent altitude; it has special significance for the instrument pilot (he may not go below this altitude unless certain conditions are satisfied), but for you, in an emergency situation, it merely represents an altitude which will clear all obstacles until you are very close to the airport. (What to do close-in will be covered in much greater detail in Chapter 10.)

Once the descent to the airport is begun, the controller will advise you of the proper altitude each mile or so. If you see that your rate of descent is falling behind (for example, the controller says "... and your altitude should now be one thousand four hundred feet" and you're still at 1,800), squeeze off another 1–2 inches of manifold pressure (or 100–200 rpm) until you catch up with the suggested glide path. In the opposite situation (when you are considerably lower than the recommended altitude), apply enough power to stop the descent, and fly level until you are once again in consonance with the controller's recommendations.

Most fixed-gear airplanes can be flown handily at cruise speed during a radar approach; you shouldn't need to change airspeed until you spot the runway. The retractables are another story, and most of them will need to be slowed down so that they don't overrun the airport when they break out of the clouds. The procedure for decelerating with safety and positive control of the aircraft is fully explained in Chapter 10.

Keeping on Course

Heading control is very important during a radar approach procedure, because the controller sees only a target on the screen; any deviations from the desired flight path will be blamed on the effect of wind, and subsequent corrective headings will serve only to increase the course error. Don't construe this to mean that controllers expect airline captain proficiency from a VFR-only pilot in an emergency situation—they know better than that—but make every effort to stay close to the assigned headings. The rudder-only method described earlier (Page 52) works beautifully, since there is no hurry involved; let the controller know that you will be making very slow turns, and your special needs will be accommodated. When you are flying the final approach portion of the procedure (descending to the airport), it's likely that you'll be requested to make some small heading changes, perhaps only five degrees or so. Here's where you should reduce the angle of bank to *five* degrees, to prevent overcontrolling and overshooting the desired heading. Remember, just enough rudder *pressure* to establish the angle of bank you want, then just enough rudder *pressure* to stop the heading indicator where you want it.

Like all the other emergency procedures under discussion, there is a great deal to be said for practicing a radar approach now and then. Because you must use Air Traffic Control facilities, and because you will tie up a controller or two for a period of time, you should choose your radar practice sessions with care and consideration. The worst time to ask for a practice approach is during one of the several "rush hours" experienced by nearly all radar-equipped terminals. Find out when traffic is at a minimum (makes sense to call the ATC office on the field and ask them when's the best time), and make your intentions clear during the initial radio conversations. Controllers are required to conduct a certain number of radar approaches to remain current and proficient in this procedure, and most of the time they'll be pleased to work you into the system.

Make your first practice a VFR exercise, so you can see what it's like, and gain an appreciation for the accuracy that can result from good controlling and good flying. Then, with a properly qualified safety pilot beside you, fly a couple of approaches under the hood; there's no better way to brush up (or develop) your IFR skills in general, and provide yourself with some almost-real experience in emergency techniques.

The pilot in command is the only judge of his ability to survive in weather conditions he observes ahead of his aircraft. When a non-IFR pilot has been operating in safe weather conditions and subsequently—for whatever reason—finds himself involved in an untenable weather situation, the near-universal solution is a 180—and a return to known, survivable conditions.

There is nothing so absolutely fundamental to a pilot as survival; and there is no objective that justifies the certain risk of an attempt to continue flight in adverse weather.

Survival is everything.

8 / *The DF Steer*

The most likely "life preserver" that ATC will throw to a VFR pilot in difficulty is, of course, radar, and it is covered in considerable detail in the previous chapter. But there may be times when you're flying in an area beyond radar coverage, or when the radar units are inoperative (they do break down on occasion, you know!), and, if you're going to get rescued, some other method will have to be employed.

Not quite so accurate, not nearly so widespread as radar, but every bit as useful when the chips are down, the network of direction-finding stations serves as a sort of backup system for locating and guiding errant pilots to a safe haven. These facilities are commonly referred to as DF stations, and the information they provide is known as a DF steer—headings to be flown to bring the aircraft over the station itself, or a nearby airport.

Basic Needs and Procedures

Very simply, the equipment consists of a VHF radio receiver in a Flight Service Station or control tower, special electronic components to analyze the signal coming from an airplane, and a display of some sort to show the operator the bearing of the aircraft from the DF facility. Whenever you transmit, your bearing can be readily determined and subsequent headings provided. Obviously, a single station can determine only in which direction you happen to be located; but combine that information with the bearing from another DF station, and the crossed bearing lines provide a fix. However your position is determined, the operator can then advise no-wind headings that should bring you to the immediate vicinity of the station; once an accurate track is established, you may even be provided with an "IFR approach" of sorts to fly you right over the airport.

A Flight Service Station specialist or a tower controller who's really on the ball will sense a problem in the first couple of transmissions from a pilot who's having trouble, and may have the DF equipment set to go by the time you 'fess up. Regardless, you should let them know right away that you need a DF steer to optimize the timely assistance of this system. You'll be instructed to key the microphone for about ten seconds at specified times, which provides the steady signal required by the ground equipment to come up with a bearing. To make sure that everybody knows who's doing what, you should end that "silent" transmission with your aircraft call sign.

A typical DF steer scenario might go like this (remember that virtually all FSS's monitor 122.2; it's a good frequency to use in this case):

You: Any station reading Cessna 1234 please reply, this is an emergency, request a DF steer.

More than likely, the nearest FSS will answer, the one which received the strongest signal when you spoke.

Them: Roger, Cessna 1234. This is Cedar Rapids Radio, do you know your position?

You: Negative. I have flown into clouds at four thousand five hundred feet somewhere in the vicinity of Waterloo, and I am not instrument-rated.

Them: Roger, Cessna 1234. Maintain your present heading and altitude, remain on this frequency, and when I tell you to transmit, hold your mike button down for ten seconds. Transmit now.

Hold down your mike button for ten seconds.

You: Cessna 1234.

Them (after a few seconds, during which they are figuring out just where you are): Roger, Cessna 1234. We have you approximately 15 miles southeast of Waterloo; turn to a heading of one five zero.

You: Cessna 1234 turning right, heading one five zero.

Them: [additional requests and instructions as required]

You: [additional answers and compliances as required to get you headed in the right direction]

Both Parties: [A huge sigh of relief when you finally catch sight of the ground, or an airport, or both]

Sometimes your transmission might be too short, or the distance so great that the quality of the signal is too poor to be used by the ground station; then the operator will ask you to transmit again. Depending on the type of equipment installed in the FSS or tower, it may be necessary for you to transmit some spoken words, or a steady "ah-h-h-h" tone; whatever the situation, the FSS person will provide precise instructions, and you must follow them to the letter for the best possible service.

The DF operator may ask you to tune in a VOR station and determine which radial you're on. This is a big help in nailing down your position, since it provides a valuable cross-check. But if your hands are full just flying the airplane and talking, let them know so that you are not distracted from your primary responsibility.

Practice DF Steers—You Can Go It Alone

A DF steer is the simplest form of navigational assistance provided by Air Traffic Control, but it has the potential of being very confusing and bewildering if you have no idea what it's like. Flight Service specialists and tower controllers need the practice, too (there's some interpretation involved in figuring out your bearing when you transmit for a steer), so it's not at all out of order to ask for a *practice* DF steer on occasion, and see how accurate they — and you — can be. You don't need a safety pilot, you don't need to mention any code words, no emergency, just ask for a "practice DF steer." Most stations will be more than happy to comply — and you'll know what it's all about if and when the real thing shows up.

The pilot in command is the only judge of his ability to survive in weather conditions he observes ahead of his aircraft. When a non-IFR pilot has been operating in safe weather conditions and subsequently—for whatever reason—finds himself involved in an untenable weather situation, the near-universal solution is a 180—and a return to known, survivable conditions.

There is nothing so absolutely fundamental to a pilot as survival; and there is no objective that justifies the certain risk of an attempt to continue flight in adverse weather.

Survival is everything.

9 / VOR Navigation

One of the premises on which this book is based is that the airplane you're flying when the emergency occurs is equipped minimally in terms of navigation gear, and for most of today's general aviation fleet, that means at least one VOR receiver. The rules require that student pilots be instructed in the fundamentals of radio navigation, but with the exception of those who go on to more detailed and comprehensive aeronautical studies, such as training for the instrument rating, VOR navigation skills don't grow much over the years. Given the shallow base of knowledge to start with, the probable atrophy of that knowledge over the years, and the stress of an emergency situation, most non-instrument pilots need a simplified procedure to get the most from their VOR equipment in a demanding set of circumstances. That's what this chapter is all about.

The Working Principles

Although VOR transmitters have different names and different frequencies, there's a common base to their operation: they all send out a constant stream of electronic energy, available to anyone whose receiver can pick up the signal. There are actually two transmitters involved, and it's the phase relationship between these two that produces a useful signal; in simplistic terms, the VOR receiver in your airplane has the capability of interpreting those signals and indicating where your airplane is in relation to the VOR station.

In effect, there are 360 electronic lines, or radials, proceeding outward from the transmitter, each one assigned a number which corresponds to its displacement from magnetic north. The 090 radial is, therefore, the imaginary line which proceeds from the transmitter due east; the 180 radial runs from the station directly south, the 225 radial goes to the southwest, and so on. The course selector (often called the omni bearing selector, or OBS) on your instrument panel allows you to select a particular radial, and when the left-right needle (the official name is course deviation indicator, or CDI) is in the center of the instrument, you're on that line.

Since a controller or FSS specialist will almost certainly ask "What radial are you on?" during the course of a "rescue" exercise, your understanding of the terminology is important. A radial is always a magnetic course *from* a VOR station. When flying away from the transmitter, the numbers used to identify both radial and course (track across the ground) are the same. For example, flying due east *from* a VOR, your course will be 090 degrees, and you are indeed on the 090 radial. But when you turn around and proceed inbound on that same radial, the course becomes the reciprocal—you are still on the 090

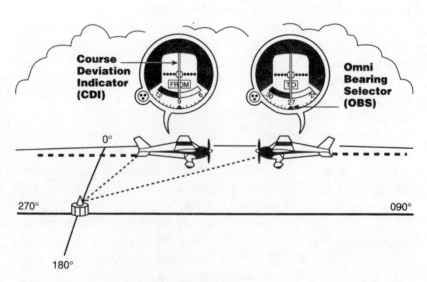

VOR-navigation instrument displays

radial, but the course is now 270. It's a simple matter of adding or subtracting 180 degrees, and it must be done whenever you are flying *to* a VOR station.

In addition to the information displayed to let you know whether you're on a particular radial or not, all VOR instrumentation provides a TO-FROM indicator. When a course is selected with the OBS knob, the appearance of TO means that if you turn the aircraft to that heading, you'll be flying toward the station. Whenever the FROM shows up, continued flight on a heading the same as the course you have selected will take you away from the transmitter. If you establish yourself on a particular radial and fly with a TO indication until you reach the station, the TO-FROM will flip-flop when you're directly above the transmitter, and will read FROM after station passage.

Instrument pilots are trained extensively in the art of interpreting the VOR displays so that they can intercept specific radials, reverse course, identify airway intersections, execute holding patterns, and perform other refinements of the art of radio navigation. But the VFR pilot who finds himself in IFR conditions should be concerned only with the most fundamental applications of VOR navigation— namely, finding out where he is in relation to the VOR and following a radial to or from the station.

Getting the Most from your VOR—When it Counts Most

The first problem—where am I?—can be very neatly resolved with the use of two VOR receivers, an aeronautical chart, pencil and straight-edge, and enough room in the cockpit to spread out the chart and draw some lines. But you're in a survival situation, and that kind of distraction from the primary job of flying the airplane is certainly not advised. Remember the discussion about head-turning and disorientation (Pages 15–22)?

Concentrate on flying, get in touch with somebody in the ATC system, and let *them* do the plotting—you're busy enough surviving.

When you've established communications with a Flight Service Station or Center, and they have at least a rough idea of your location, they'll have you tune the frequency for a nearby VOR and ask you on which radial you're located. Rotate the OBS until the left-right needle is *centered*, and the TO-FROM indicator shows FROM, and tell the folks on the ground what number you see under the OBS index; they'll take it from there.

If you're *really* lost, in unfamiliar country without even a hint of possible VOR frequencies in the vicinity, and unable to reach anyone on the radio for help, tune your VOR receiver to 112.0 and start up the scale—112.1, 112.2, etc. When you find a frequency that brings the needles and pointers and flags to life *and which produces either a clear Morse code signal or a recorded voice to identify the station,* turn the OBS until the needle centers with a TO indication, and fly that heading. Climb if you can to maintain a usable signal and better your chances of establishing communications. (The VOR signal is good for approximately 40 nautical miles over flat terrain but is subject to the same line-of-sight restrictions as VHF voice communications.) If you can get close to a VOR, there will be a Flight Service Station—and *help*—within radio range.

Lifesaver: The VOR Fix

If you are in complete control of the airplane and have it trimmed so that it will fly hands-off for long periods of time, or if you are enjoying the luxuries of an autopilot or wing leveler, there is a way to nail down your position more accurately once you're on the way to a VOR. Check the chart for another VOR station off to the right or left (the ideal would be a station off either wing tip; the closer it is to a 90-degree "cut" the better your fix will be), determine which of its radials you're on, then draw both lines on your chart—the radial on which you're flying, and the one you're crossing. Where the lines cross is where you are, or were, just a few minutes ago. A second VOR receiver comes in mighty handy for this procedure, but you can accomplish the objective with only one radio—it just takes a minute or two longer.

It's quite possible that the extra work involved in a two-VOR fix may be more than you can handle in an emergency, so don't attempt this procedure unless you're having no trouble flying the airplane. When in doubt about your ability to maintain controlled flight (is anything else really important?), *let the controllers do the navigating for you.* Stick to that primary VOR station like glue.

"Cut and Try" — it Works

Correcting for the effects of wind is just as much a feature of good navigation when using VOR as it is with any other system, but the VOR panel display takes all the work out of it. Once on a radial, drift correction is simply a matter of keeping the left-right needle centered. At the outset, turn to the *heading* which corresponds to the OBS reading you see when the needle centers with a TO reading. As soon as you detect movement of the left-right indicator, turn 10 degrees in the appropriate direction—whichever way the needle moves. If that happens to be enough of a crab angle to effectively counteract the wind, the needle will stop moving. You might hit the right combination the first time, but more than likely you'll have to cut and try a bit; for instance, 10 degrees into the wind may prove to be too much, and the needle will come back to center and keep on going, off to the other

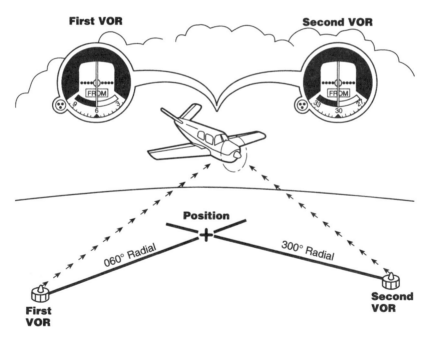

Determining position by plotting radials from two VOR transmitters

side of center. When this happens, return to the original heading (same as the OBS setting) and wait until the needle once again centers, then put in only 5 degrees of wind correction.

On the other hand, should the original 10 degrees not be enough to keep the airplane on course, the left-right needle will continue to move away from center. As soon as you notice this situation, get busy, because you're moving away from your intended course at a rapid rate; turn *30* degrees back toward the center line and hold it until the needle centers. Now try reducing the correction to 20 degrees, and watch the needle. Sooner or later you'll come across a heading that will balance the force of the wind, and you can proceed to the station on course.

As you get close to the transmitter, the sensitivity of the indicator increases rather remarkably, and the left-right needle will begin to move erratically back and forth across the instrument. Hang in there— stay with the heading that worked most of the way in, and you will cross the station in fine shape. When you're on the other side, the left-right needle will slow its oscillations, and eventually settle down, more than likely very close to center once again.

A Great Nav Aid, But...

While VOR has many good things going for it—lots of stations scattered around the country, straight-line accuracy, relatively simple presentation—it's only as good as the operator who sets it up and does the interpretation. There are a couple of common errors which you should be able to avoid simply by knowing about them. First, make sure you are working with the station you *think* you have tuned; it's not at all difficult to get a strong signal from a station farther away, and the TO-FROM and left-right indications seem proper (these illusions will be *very* strong when you're faced with an emergency and you want so badly to believe what you see). This source of error can be eliminated by forming the tune-and-identify habit; don't move your hand from the receiver until you have turned up the audio and are certain of the Morse code (sometimes a vocal ident) that comes out of the speaker. All the aeronautical charts have the Morse code printed clearly along with the VOR frequency, and it will be transmitted slowly enough for you to figure it out.

Error number two involves the heading-OBS relationship; whenever you are intending to fly *toward* a VOR station, be certain that the word TO appears in the TO-FROM indicator. Anything else indicates that something is bad wrong, and the opposite is true when your intent is to leave the station behind.

Finally, all your work is for nothing if your VOR receiver has developed gross inaccuracies over a period of time. There are simple methods of checking VOR receivers for accuracy — these checks are required every 30 days for legal operation in the IFR system. Most accurate is the VOT, or VOR test signal. It's a "phony" VOR transmitter set up on an airport (usually the larger ones), and which transmits only one radial — the 360 radial. So no matter where your airplane is located, the VOR receivers on board think they are *north* of the station, and when you select 360 on the OBS, the left-right needle should center, with a FROM indication. To check the accuracy, rotate the OBS until the left-right needle *does* center, and the reading on the OBS must be within ±4 degrees of 360. A similar but opposite check confirms the receiver's accuracy with an OBS selection of 180.

Another means of checking your VOR equipment consists of a designated ground checkpoint, usually indicated by a sign on a taxiway or ramp, and telling you that at this spot the left-right needle should center with the OBS on such-and-such a setting; again, the allowable IFR tolerance is ±4 degrees, and if your receiver displays a larger error, it's time to put it in the shop for recalibration. Trying to navigate with out-of-tolerance VOR receivers is like a surgeon operating with a dull knife.

Flying a VOR Approach

Up to this point we've been concerned only with the technique you'll require to locate yourself, figure out which way to go to get to the VOR transmitter, and do it. But what if there's no radar available, no Flight Service Station handy to provide you with a DF steer? What if you arrive over the VOR and find that you're still in the clouds? What *now*, VFR pilot?

An unhappy situation, to be sure, but not one which can't be resolved. It's too much to ask VFR-limited pilots to carry published

VOR approach procedure charts around with them, but there's always someone in the ATC system who knows (or who can find out in a hurry) what the pertinent numbers are. Those numbers, of course, being the correct radial, the appropriate minimum altitudes, and, for most procedures, the distance from VOR station to airport. There are numerous cases on record in which a nonpilot — someone who knew next to nothing about the airplane — was talked down to a safe landing after the left-seater suffered some sort of incapacitation; if that can be done with someone who started with zero knowledge and skill, it stands to reason that a *pilot* who can maintain control of the airplane in IFR conditions can be "talked through" an IFR approach procedure. It's not nearly as complicated as you might think.

VOR, Where Are You?

There are two basic configurations for VOR approach procedures: one in which the transmitter is located right on the airport, and one in which it's necessary to fly to the VOR, then proceed on a specified radial for a certain distance to the airport. In both cases the charts will indicate a safe minimum altitude for the final segment of the approach, an altitude which will usually bring you to within 300–500 feet of the ground. For the purposes of this discussion, we'll assume a worst-case scenario: there is no radar, no navigational help of any kind available except someone on the ground who can supply the proper radials, altitudes, and distances. We'll also assume that a VOR is located on the airport, that you are approaching the transmitter on a radial other than the one published for the approach, and that your altitude is higher than the prescribed minimum. Not enough of a challenge? Let's throw in a low-ceiling, low-visibility weather situation, one that will force you to descend to minimum altitude and get to the VOR not more than a half mile or so off course.

That "someone on the ground" is going to be, quite literally, your savior during this procedure, so just as soon as it becomes apparent that you will need to fly the approach in order to save the day, *insist* that the controller to whom you're talking stay with you and be prepared to furnish all the information you might need.

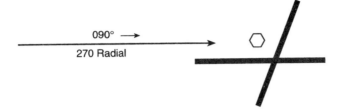

Figure A

For the time being, forget altitude and airspeed considerations, concentrate on getting to the VOR, establishing the aircraft on the proper radial, and then navigating to the airport.

Figure A shows an airport with a VOR installed between the runways, a not uncommon situation. Although "all roads (radials) lead to Rome"—and if you were able to fly to the VOR you'd certainly be in sight of the airport—the 270 radial has been designated the final approach course, the one on which you can safely descend to the minimum altitude if the ceiling is low or the visibility very poor. If you find yourself proceeding toward the station on or near this radial, there's not much procedure to be accomplished, but let's continue our worst-case scenario and have you approach the station on some other radial. Now, you've got to get turned around in order to let down to the minimum altitude prescribed for the final approach segment of the procedure. There's a simple, cookbook method to use, one which involves a minimum of maneuvering on your part, and one which will put you on course, inbound, just like the real IFR pilots.

The dashed lines in Figure B indicate several typical approaches to the VOR and show that the first thing you must do upon reaching the station is *turn in the shortest direction to the outbound heading*, in this case 270 degrees. (There's ample opportunity to get all messed up in the numbers here, so be sure you understand exactly what your ground-bound helper has told you; be certain that one of you is not talking radials while the other is referring to headings.) For airplane A it's a left turn, airplane B should turn to the right, C to the left, and D to the right. The objective of this maneuver is to place your airplane on an outbound course parallel to the final approach course, so that

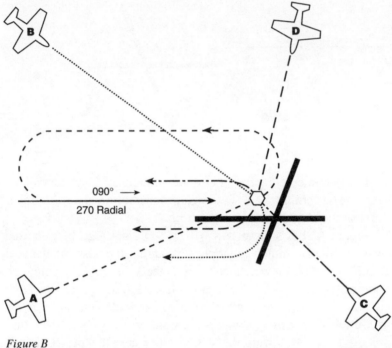

Figure B

you can turn around, descend when it's safe to do so, and return to the station at an altitude that will permit you to catch sight of the airport in time to land. The complete maneuver is illustrated for airplane A; the others would fly similar tracks on appropriate sides of the 270 radial.

When that first turn is complete (take your time, use rudder pressure just like before to establish a 10-degree bank), *reset the OBS to the outbound course*—in the example, 270. You will now have a positive indication of which way to turn when the time comes to reverse course and fly back to the station; if the left-right needle lies to the right of center when you set 270 in the OBS, that's where the inbound course lies, and vice versa when the needle swings to the left.

Because of the relatively large-radius turn produced by the 10-degree angle of bank, you may well see the word TO when you set the OBS to 270—you're still on the wrong side of the station, or in this case still *east* of the VOR. Keep flying westbound, and when the TO-

FROM *does* change to FROM (or if it shows FROM when you complete the first turn), *take note of the time*; you will need to fly outbound for three minutes, to provide enough time to get oriented, turn around, and descend to the safe minimum altitude.

At the completion of the first turn, aircraft C and D will wind up very close to the final approach course (absent a strong north or south wind), and aircraft A and B will be considerably further displaced. In either case, at the end of three minutes outbound you should *reset the OBS to the inbound course*—in the example, 090—and begin your turn to the east (or whatever heading is appropriate for the procedure you might be flying). For the sake of simplification, *continue the turn until you are in fact heading due east;* once again, the left-right needle will show you clearly which way to turn to get back on the final approach course. Needle left? Turn left—and vice versa.

The Needle Knows, But...

If the gods are smiling upon you this day (well, smiling more than they were a while ago when you got into this mess!), the left-right needle will center at the same time you roll out on a heading of 090—but don't count on it. To correct back to course, turn in the appropriate direction no more than 30 degrees, and hold that new heading until the needle slides back to center. If the movement of the left-right indicator is very slow, or if it seems to be glued to the side of the instrument case, alter your expectations a bit; you will not fly directly overhead but will pass the station with the VOR on the same side to which the needle is displaced. Not the most precise VOR navigation in the world, but it should put you close enough to the station (and therefore the airport) to see it in all but the worst visibility conditions.

Suppose the left-right needle slides across the center while you are still in the turn toward the east? No matter, continue the turn and take up a corrective heading after you have rolled out, settled down, and gotten your ducks in a row. Now, when everything is in place again, turn 30 degrees toward the needle and hold it until the needle either centers or you pass the station.

At those airports where the VOR is *not* located on the field but at some distance away (this may vary from a mile or two to perhaps twenty or more), the same procedure just discussed will get you lined up on the approach radial, the only difference being in the post-station technique. As before, the heading which brought you to the VOR on course—or nearly so—will take you away from the station just as handily. You must obtain the time required to fly from VOR to airport (this information is contained on the approach procedure charts, and can be supplied by your friend on the ground), and it becomes important to notice when the TO-FROM meter changes indications; that's station passage, and you must start keeping track of the time. A digital watch or timer really earns its keep here.

In summary, then, a simplified procedure for flying a survival approach using a VOR station:

- Contact someone on the ground who can lay his hands on the published approach procedure for the airport you intend to use, and determine the final approach course.

- If you are on or near the final-approach radial, find out the minimum safe altitude on that radial, and descend to it as soon as it's safe to do so. If you don't have any idea of your distance from the VOR, you may have to fly all the way to the station and get turned around before a safe descent can be made.

- When station passage is confirmed (TO-FROM changes to FROM), turn in the shortest direction to the outbound heading.

- When the first turn is complete, reset the OBS to the outbound course and notice the displacement of the left-right needle.

- Continue outbound for three minutes, then begin a turn toward the needle to get back on course inbound. Reset the OBS to the inbound course.

- At the completion of this turn, correct back to course if necessary. Use a maximum 30-degree correction angle, always in the direction indicated by the displacement of the left-right needle.

- When the left-right needle is centered, descend to the safe minimum altitude, and fly to the station. If the VOR lies short of the airport, continue on the appropriate radial until the field comes into sight. Be sure to obtain the time-to-airport information, and start your timer when you're over the VOR transmitter.

So endeth a thumbnail sketch of basic navigational procedures using the ubiquitous VOR. There's much more involved, of course, in using this NAVAID to its fullest, but this bare-bones technique coupled with some practice on your part should make the VOR a useful navigational tool in an emergency. Experiment with VOR (simulate IFR conditions with a hood whenever possible) and find out what you and the system can do. When the day of reckoning arrives, your familiarity with VOR will boost your confidence and ability to fly out of trouble.

The pilot in command is the only judge of his ability to survive in weather conditions he observes ahead of his aircraft. When a non-IFR pilot has been operating in safe weather conditions and subsequently—for whatever reason—finds himself involved in an untenable weather situation, the near-universal solution is a 180—and a return to known, survivable conditions.

There is nothing so absolutely fundamental to a pilot as survival; and there is no objective that justifies the certain risk of an attempt to continue flight in adverse weather.

Survival is everything.

10 / Approach and Landing

Once located and pointed in the right direction, the VFR pilot trying to survive in IFR conditions still has a formidable task to accomplish, assuming a weather situation at the airport that will require some sort of navigation procedure in order to get the airplane close enough to the runway to see it and land safely.

Our attention thus far has focused on the pilot techniques for level flight at cruise airspeed, and for executing safe, gentle turns. But the airplane is a three-dimensional machine, and navigating successfully through any kind of approach procedure (radar-assisted or do-it-yourself with the help of VOR) includes consideration of the vertical dimension as well; sooner or later you must descend to the lowest safe altitude provided by the GOG (guy or gal on ground).

Preparation for a descent in actual weather conditions should be started while you are still some distance from the point at which the descent will begin—perhaps five minutes, at least, to give you time to adjust to the new sounds and feelings and control responses. The first step in the descent procedure for a VFR-limited pilot is to establish level flight at a new, lower airspeed; this will slow the progression of events and increase the effective visibility when you break out of the clouds. In a low-visibility situation, you are flying at the peak of a gray cone, its fuzzy edges reaching to the ground at the outer limits of your visibility. The slower you travel, the slower the cone moves across the ground, and the more time you have to perceive and identify objects which grow out of the murk—objects such as power lines, mountains, TV towers, other airplanes, and of course *airports*; all of which you'd like to avoid except the last.

Letting Down

When slowdown time comes, when it's time to prepare for the descent, you may well undo all your good work up to this point by rushing into a new condition of flight. *Take your time!* With the airplane trimmed hands-off at cruise airspeed, very slowly *squeeze* the throttle until you see a power reduction of 100 rpm or 1 inch of manifold pressure (a slight touch of left rudder pressure will be necessary to control the heading). Since you have deprived the airplane of some of the power required to maintain level flight, there can be only one result—the airplane will begin to descend, as the trimmed tail pitches the nose down almost imperceptibly to maintain the airspeed you've programmed. If you take no action at this point, the airplane will continue to descend *at the cruise airspeed*, but that's not the object here. Just as soon as you notice the altimeter hand beginning to leave its level-flight reading, adjust the elevator trim to stop the descent—it won't take much—and you have reprogrammed the airplane for a new, slightly lower airspeed.

You're moving in the right direction now, so once again reduce power *by no more than 100 rpm or 1 inch of manifold pressure* (if you try to do this any more rapidly, you'll overcontrol and wind up with a porpoising airplane, and you won't like it!), retrim when you see the altimeter slipping, and continue this process in increments until the airspeed settles at the number you normally use in a VFR traffic pattern. It's a good compromise speed, one that will provide good control and response to changes in power settings, yet won't be so fast that you'll miss the airport at the end of the approach.

Squeeze Play

With the airplane slowed and trimmed at the new airspeed, a safe, positive, hands-off descent can be accomplished by the simple expedient of reducing power further. Airspeed will remain very close to the trimmed value, the airplane will pitch down just enough to maintain the trim airspeed, and your rate of descent will depend on the amount of power you take away. A good rule of thumb: at approach airspeeds, airplanes with fixed-pitch propellers will descend roughly 100 feet per minute for each 100 rpm of power reduction; those airplanes with controllable-pitch props will descend about 100 feet per minute for each inch of manifold pressure reduction. In any event, change the power setting very slowly (*squeeze!*), and don't reduce power more than 500 rpm or 5 inches; using that as a limit, you won't end up with a high rate of descent which, for the untrained pilot, can very easily upset the controllability applecart—something you definitely don't need right now.

As you approach the desired altitude (furnished by the controller, who will be reading it from an approach chart, or perhaps some other publication or display which gives him the safe minimum altitude for your location) slowly *squeeze* the throttle back to the pre-descent level-flight setting. You may well have to make minor power adjustments to maintain level flight at the lower altitude, but *don't touch the trim!* When you arrive at a power setting sufficient for level flight at the new altitude, all the stability and control you enjoyed at cruise will remain, but at a slower speed.

There's a special technique for the retractables. In addition to respecting the airspeed limitations of the gear-lowering system (wheel well doors and retraction mechanisms have a way of coming loose when they are exposed to the air pressure of very high speeds), one of the major concerns in an emergency situation like this is *pilot* overload; it's bad business to try to do more than one thing at a time, no matter how sharp you think you are, or how well you've done up until now. Every camel's back will break under *some* load, so don't pile on any more straws.

Pilots of retractable-gear airplanes should slow down their machines in level flight (again, well in advance of the descent point) using the power-trim, power-trim, power-trim technique just explained. *Then*, when it's time to head for lower altitudes, leave the throttle right where it is, *lower the gear*, and watch a feat of aerodynamic magic take place before your very eyes. The increased drag of the lowered wheels will tend to slow the airplane down a bit, but the elevator, trimmed for a specific airspeed, will pitch the nose down just enough to maintain that speed. You've just proved that the word DOWN on the gear switch also applies to altitude, and most light airplanes will float serenely downhill at a rate of approximately 500 feet per minute — safe, comfortable, positive.

Just before reaching the new altitude, leave the gear down and *squeeze* the power handle forward until the altimeter hands stop moving; you'll probably need to add about 5 inches of manifold pressure (there aren't many fixed-pitch retractable-gear airplanes, but if yours fits that category, the power increase will be about 500 rpm). The bottom line is this: add just enough power to maintain level flight and just enough rudder pressure to make the heading indicator stand still. There should be no need to think about the landing gear again on this flight.

Regardless of the kind of airplane you're flying when faced with an approach in actual weather, you must limit your actions to one at a time. No matter how anxious you are to get on the ground and get this nightmare over with, don't be tempted to overstep the bounds of your capabilities by trying to do more than one thing at a time. If a descent is called for, descend straight ahead; when you need to make a turn, either let it wait until you've stopped descending, or re-establish level flight before you start to change heading. There are so many illusory traps involved, *traps you have not been trained to avoid*, that you will be treading on very thin ice if you try to combine turns with climbs or descents. Tell the controller; he'll adjust to your limitations as required.

There are so many possible combinations of conditions that might prevail at the very end of your survival exercise that it's impossible to provide a single procedure for the landing phase. For example, you might break out of the clouds and/or low visibility directly over the airport too high to make a safe landing on any of its runways; or you might spot the airport from several miles out, in visibility conditions good enough for you to proceed as if you were completing a routine VFR trip; or you might have gotten to the airport with radar guidance or your own VOR navigation, but discover that you're lined up with a runway with a strong crosswind or tailwind component.

UNIVERSITY OF WALES AIR SQUADRON

R.A.F.V.R.

AR ESGYLL DYSG

Beggars Can't Be Choosers

Whatever the situation when the airport comes into view, keep in mind that you have just extricated yourself from a serious emergency, and that you should remain in "emergency" mode until the wheels come to a stop. You *don't* want to fly back into the clouds and have to go through that trauma all over again, so it's important to get the airplane on the ground in one piece; that may require accepting a strong crosswind or tailwind and taking your chances with a low-velocity mishap on the ground. Let's face an immutable fact: your chances of walking away unhurt are much, much better in a run-off-the-pavement type of accident than if you put the airplane into the ground as the result of a stall-spin while you're trying to execute the high-performance maneuvers needed to line up with a "better" runway in low-visibility or high-wind conditions.

If you feel it's necessary to maneuver the airplane into a more favorable position for the landing approach (and who could possibly be a better judge of that need than you?), don't ruin the day by changing anything other than heading; use the same 10-degree bank that has kept you from harm, and turn until you're lined up where you want to be. Chances are very good that your altitude will be rather low at this point, so leave the throttle right where it is, the engine producing enough power to maintain level flight at pattern airspeed. When you are on a final approach that looks good, begin *squeezing* the throttle back to a setting that will produce a glide to the runway, flaps as required or desired as in a normal VFR landing — which this has now become.

Pilots who are not trained to adjust rapidly to the changing visual scene at the end of an instrument approach will usually fly a "hot" final — with the airspeed remaining at or near normal cruise or normal pattern speed until they're almost on the ground. There's no doubt a strong subconscious input based on the urgent need to "get this thing on the ground," plus the pervasive feeling that airspeed is safety — if some is good, more is better. True only up to a point; a high-speed final requires sudden and drastic power/flap/trim changes if a "normal" landing is to be completed, and that may be more than you can handle at this time. The weather situation which caused all this unhappiness may well be one which has also produced some precipitation, and a wet runway just makes things worse when touchdown finally does occur.

Your best procedure, the most effective mental attitude to establish when the runway comes into view, is to shift your aviator gears into "normal" just as soon as you can. Turn if you must, but not one degree more than is absolutely necessary; if you find it impossible to land on the first attempt, set up a normal pattern if you can. The more nearly you can make things look the same way they do in an everyday flying situation, the more likely you'll be able to conclude your survival exercise with success.

Only if You Must, But...

For an instrument pilot, the aeronautical maneuver known as a missed approach is a rather normal sort of thing. It arises from one of two situations: a cloud ceiling or visibility restriction prevents acquiring the runway visually when the lowest altitude/runway proximity is reached, or the pilot has botched the navigational job and finds himself grossly off course.

For a VFR-limited pilot in an IFR survival situation, however, a missed approach is perhaps the most *abnormal* operation that might be contemplated. In addition to forcing you to undertake yet another change in power setting and condition of flight, a missed approach caused by weather so inclement that you can't spot the airport when you fly over it means that you must continue walking the tightrope of IFR operations until you can find an airport with visibility good enough for landing. You've had a large problem, got it almost solved, now you've got to fly through the clouds all over again. It's bound to be psychologically trying.

Weather systems that produce these unflyable conditions are usually adequately forecast, and it isn't likely that many VFR-limited types will venture forth when the low-ceiling, low-visibility writing has been on the wall long enough for them to have been warned about it. But it would be unrealistic and unfair to assume that this could *never* happen, and fail to include in a book like this at least some basic procedures and techniques to cope with the possibility of having to climb back to a safe altitude and go somewhere else, or come back for another try. Don't execute a missed-approach maneuver unless it's absolutely necessary, but if you're forced into it, here are some guidelines.

What Goes Up, *Must*

The most important part of *any* missed-approach procedure is the transition from level flight to a climb; when you're down close to the ground and run out of visibility, all the hazards lie below and the first move *must* be vertical. If you have set up the airplane as suggested—at normal VFR traffic pattern airspeed, trimmed hands-off, gear down if it's a retractable, just enough power to maintain level flight—the initial pilot action to enter a climb depends on the type of airplane you're flying. The fixed-gear pilot need only increase power to maximum (*squeeze* the throttle!), simultaneously increase right rudder pressure as necessary to keep the heading indicator from moving, and watch the altimeter begin to indicate a climb. The elevator, faithful to the airspeed you programmed into it a long way back, will react to the initial speed increase by pitching the nose up to keep the airspeed where it belongs, and the result will be a steady, positive climb—precisely what you want.

Those with retractable-gear airplanes have an even simpler task at missed-approach time. Recall that the additional drag of the landing gear was used to initiate a descent, then power was increased as required to hold the airplane in level flight *with the gear still extended.* Level, with gear hanging out, you are now flying an airplane which is *over*powered for level flight except for the drag of the landing gear; it stands to reason and the laws of aerodynamics that if you retract the landing gear with no change in power setting, there will be an excess of power, and something has to give. That something will be altitude, and when you move the gear switch or handle to the UP position, the airplane will gently pitch up a bit, airspeed will remain right where it was, and the altimeter will begin moving steadily upward. With one stroke (and no rudder pressure changes because you haven't changed the power setting), you have transitioned from level flight to climb and are moving safely away from the ground. This technique won't produce a dazzling climb, but it will be positive and safe.

If at First You Don't Succeed...

The scenario from this point on depends entirely on the situation, and once again, there are so many variables that a simple, universal solution to the problem is impossible. If your missed approach was caused by failure (no matter whose) to get close enough to the ground to be clear of clouds or visibility restrictions, and everyone involved is reasonably confident that another try will produce success, by all means have at it again. If you're being radar-vectored or guided by a DF station, you will be directed to a safe altitude and given a series of headings intended to put you in line with the runway for your second attempt. If you have done the job solo, navigating with your VOR equipment, there's no choice but to fly directly back to the VOR (turn the OBS until the needle centers, with a TO indication; keep the left-right needle centered until TO changes to FROM) and employ the VOR approach procedures discussed in Chapter 9.

Pilot *in Command*, It's Now Up To You—*Only* You

In another situation, suppose that the airport to which you have been directed turns out to be totally "socked in," unusable because of low visibility or ceiling, and it's clear that further attempts will not only increase your frustration and further deplete your shallow reservoir of IFR skills, it will also hasten the inexorable problem of fuel exhaustion. Just as soon as you determine (or are assured by a knowledgeable person on the ground) that the chances of a successful landing here are slim to none, begin the alternate-selection process. You—and *only* you—can make the final decision to fly somewhere else or stay here and take your chances, but each delay cuts deeper into your fuel supply. And no matter how indecisive you may be, no matter how long you put it off, when the engine draws that last drop of gasoline from the tanks, you will be playing ball with an entirely different set of rules—all options have just been withdrawn.

Summarizing, here are some key points involved in a successful instrument approach and landing:

• Slow the airplane to normal VFR traffic pattern airspeed ahead of the point at which you will have to descend. Reduce power in very small increments, retrim to maintain altitude, reduce power again, retrim, and so on until the desired airspeed is obtained.

• To enter a descent, reduce power by not more than 500 rpm or 5 inches of manifold pressure, rudder pressure as required to hold heading constant. Level off by replacing the power you took away, or, if a rather large altitude change took place, just enough power to maintain level flight.

• If yours is a retractable-gear airplane, get it slowed down, then initiate the descent by lowering the wheels. Level off by adding enough power to maintain level flight, leaving the landing gear extended. Further descent is accomplished by a power reduction of approximately 5 inches of manifold pressure.

• Maintain traffic pattern airspeed and level flight until the landing runway is in sight, at which time the landing glide can be set up by reducing power, adding flaps as required for a normal landing.

• If circling of any magnitude is necessary to get lined up with the runway, do it at the old familiar 10-degree bank angle, with no further descent until you are lined up for landing.

• When in doubt, land on the runway you're lined up with when you break out of the clouds. Even a strong crosswind or tailwind which results in the airplane going off the runway is better than an out-of-control crash while trying to maneuver for a "better" landing direction.

• Make all your maneuvers as near to normal as possible once you have gained sight of the ground. This is no time for experimentation.

• Avoid a missed approach. But if it becomes necessary, start climbing by either *squeezing* the throttle to full power (if yours is a fixed-pitch, fixed-gear airplane), or by simply raising the landing gear if you're flying a retractable. Execute no turns until everything has settled down and the airplane is climbing positively away from the ground. Then climb straight ahead unless a turn is absolutely imperative to miss an obstacle. Let the folks on the other end of the microphone know what's going on and what you want to do next. They'll help by supplying information, but the decision has got to be yours.

• Don't get into this situation in the first place!

The pilot in command is the only judge of his ability to survive in weather conditions he observes ahead of his aircraft. When a non-IFR pilot has been operating in safe weather conditions and subsequently—for whatever reason—finds himself involved in an untenable weather situation, the near-universal solution is a 180—and a return to known, survivable conditions.

There is nothing so absolutely fundamental to a pilot as survival; and there is no objective that justifies the certain risk of an attempt to continue flight in adverse weather.

Survival is everything.

11 / Why Not Get an Instrument Rating?

There's an aviation training film that goes to almost macabre lengths to make its point...that *humans cannot maintain their orientation in clouds unless they are trained to utilize the instrument indications.* One segment of the film includes the actual tape recording of a light-twin pilot who found himself on top of overcast and requested permission to descend through the clouds to a landing. When the controller asked if he were instrument-rated, the pilot replied, "I have maybe eighteen hours of IFR, but have not got the rating as of yet." He lost control within a few seconds of cloud penetration and crashed shortly thereafter.

In another weather-involved accident, the pilot was asked about his instrument qualifications: "Negative. I, ah, have had about ten hours of IFR..." This pilot also became disoriented, rolled the airplane over on its back, and subsequently pulled it apart during the recovery attempt.

As the airplanes we fly in general aviation become more and more capable of getting us into adverse weather conditions, complete pilot-ATC system compatibility is going to become a necessity if we are to get the most out of those expensive flying machines. There's just one way to get the job done right: get an instrument rating. The fabled IFR ticket, the great American aviation dream, right? Apparently wrong, because there are thousands of pilots who accept the restrictions of fair-weather flying.

Suppose that this came to pass: "As of midnight next Thursday, no one is allowed to drive an automobile in weather conditions that require windshield wipers unless he has been a licensed driver for two years, has been through a special course of instruction, and has proved to an examiner that he is competent and safe under those conditions." A law like that would stop the motoring public in its tracks—for a very short time. Oh, there'd be goose-drowning days when only the professional drivers would be on the road, and some of the Sunday-only drivers would decide it's less trouble to stay home on soggy Sabbaths than to go through a rain-training course. But the general response to such a ridiculous law would be overwhelming and would reflect the need for unrestricted automotive utility; the sidewalk wouldn't be long enough to hold the lines that would form in front of the "rain rating" office.

An aviator can't fly in certain kinds of weather unless he's accumulated at least 125 hours of pilot time, passed an FAA knowledge exam and a flight check. But the analogy comes apart at an interesting seam ... the IFR laws are already on the books, have been for lo these many years, and still the general-aviation community has definitely not knocked down the FAA's doors in a rush to become weather-capable. Hie yourself hence to the nearest pilots' lounge when the weather is holding just below legal VFR ("...visibility two and a half miles in haze ...") and you'll likely behold a group of very frustrated flyers. They jump up every time the teletypewriter starts clacking, in hopes that the latest reports signal a break in the weather. You'll have to stand in line at the telephone, because the VFR-limited folks are calling the tower, Approach Control, the Flight Service Station, and the local ombudsman, trying to get somebody to conjure up some fly-able weather. They should run—not walk—to the nearest flight school and get an instrument rating.

There are at Least Six Good Reasons

The best reason is probably money, or the lack thereof. Instrument training is expensive. You've got to put in at least 40 hours of IFR time, and although some of that can be logged as you go about your business, it's 40 times whatever it costs you to fly per hour. The dollars that you pour into the instrument rating can be lessened somewhat by using a simulator for some of the procedural work, but that's not the real world, and the rules insist on a bare minimum of 15 hours in an airplane with an instructor; it's doubtful he'll work for nothing. Figure the full 40 hours as inflight instructional time, and the practice hours you can slip into the program with just a safety pilot in the right seat (he *will* work for nothing) will help reduce the overall cost. On the way to the rating, don't forget to set aside some funds to cover your preparation for the FAA Knowledge Exam.

Another oft-quoted reason for not getting an instrument rating is the time involved. (People who are busy enough to need the utility that an IFR ticket affords find it very difficult to separate time and money. When an hour away from the grindstone reduces income and also runs up a bill at the airport, it costs you double.) On top of the sheer number of hours that it takes to jump through all of the Part 61 hoops to get where you're going (weather delays, instructor can't make it today, your business schedule interferes now and then, airplane gets bent), learning to fly instruments is very much a skill-developing course — that means you'll have to go back and relearn some of the last lesson, and the farther apart they're spaced, the more relearning you'll need. The ideal would be to enroll in a fly-every-day program, but there goes the vacation, or three weeks' production at the very least.

Some pilots hesitate to open the instrument door because of aircraft and equipment requirements. You can't take just any old flying machine and charge off into the IFR world; you need dependable and accurate attitude instruments and communications gear that must be checked at frequent intervals. Any way you slice it, it's going to cost more to maintain an IFR airplane — there's reason number one again. Although you won't find it specified in the rules of the air, there's absolutely no sane way to operate on instruments without a complete set of en route and approach charts; easy to understand and even easier to use, the paperwork of instrument flying costs money and requires some of your time to keep it up to date. An old sectional can get you confused; an old instrument chart can get you dead.

It's only a piece of plastic that fits in your fist, or a black button on the end of a boom, but there are people who are convinced that a microphone is a full house of air traffic controllers, airline captains, and other general aviation pilots lying in wait for the airborne bloopers.

It's controllers who cause the greatest concern, especially among low-time pilots; ATC seems to be the whole United States government wrapped up in one voice. Take a chance on missing a clearance, messing up a readback, or making a full position report? No way. For some, the ATC system is just too intimidating to even consider IFR training.

And those pilots who are turned off by currency requirements may decide that six hours of instrument time and six approaches in six months or face another checkride is more than they want to fool around with.

The sixth reason for not getting an instrument rating makes more sense than all the others combined. Pilots who intend nothing more than an occasional afternoon of fair-weather touch-and-go exercises or pleasure trips, which impose no economic or social penalty when weather pulls the VFR plug, have no *need* for IFR qualification. There'll be another day: why bother learning a skill that will never be used? The time and money would be much better spent becoming a more proficient fair-weather flyer.

Number Six is Excused: The Rest of You, Read On

If the lack of instrument capability hits you right in the pocketbook, you have ample justification for the expense of IFR training. Even if you don't use your airplane for business, weather limitations have probably cost you money. It doesn't take many unplanned nights in expensive hotels or more than a few unscheduled restaurant meals to equal the cost of a couple of hours of IFR instruction. And if you and your spouse happen to be the kind of people who can only be entertained by shopping, look out—you'll go through the price of an instrument course in one afternoon if you have the misfortune to get stuck in a high-rent district.

Suppose the lousy weather that was forecast to improve by noon stretches on into the evening, and hours of below-VFR conditions drag on into days—you've got to get back to work, so it's either pay someone else to bring the bird home or buy an airline ticket. Either way, you lose the price of a one-way ticket. And when you elect the airline route, *you* get home but the airplane is still in Steubenville.

Getting ready for the knowledge examination will take some

dollars, for books and materials and time spent in study. The problem with self-preparation lies in its aimlessness—the body of knowledge is too vast for undirected study. Since you're going to spend some money, spend it where it will do you the most good; there are formal classroom courses, self-teaching programs and computerized instruction. Take your pick.

So if you depend on your airplane, reason number one (money) should not be a deterrent. While you're looking at the cost of IFR training, check with your insurance agent; you may get a pleasant surprise when the FAA types "instrument" on your pilot certificate. A lower premium reflects the insurance carrier's recognition of your new higher level of proficiency in the air. You've gotten better and the training pays for itself; how can you beat a deal like that?

Time spent in instrument training (reason number two) is time wasted if the lessons are too far apart, or if you bite off more concentrated work than your mind can chew. Learning to fly on instruments is a lot more than just keeping the airplane right side up—there are enough other things to do that you've got to give your poor tired brain a chance to unboggle now and then. There are few pilots who can stand more than an hour and a half, sometimes two hours of IFR work, at a time—when the mind reaches saturation under the hood, it simply short-circuits; and that's the end of meaningful training for that session, possibly for that day.

A good flight instructor will set up a flight schedule that has you in the air or in the simulator as frequently as possible, but not more often than you can handle. Don't expect to become an instrument pilot next week, because IFR savvy can't be injected; it involves a lot of seasoning and maturing in the ATC system, and it doesn't happen overnight. Give yourself plenty of time, and don't work against a deadline.

The amount of equipment and the type of airplane are probably the most open-ended decisions you'll have to make with regard to instrument flying. If all you're concerned about beating is the occasional two-and-a-half-mile morning haze, there's nothing wrong with bare-minimum equipment in a single-engine airplane. As your level of involvement increases, the equipment should improve in quality and sophistication. Your best bet is to chat with people who are operating at the level you intend—find out what black boxes they have, and which ones they'd rather have if they could do it over again.

Same thing with charts for instrument work; there are only two approved sources, and you'll find the house of aviation pretty evenly divided on this score. Get some samples of each, talk to the people who use them, and then make up your own mind.

The fourth reason for not getting an instrument rating (mike fright) can be very neatly dispatched by an instructor who understands the peculiar mental chemistry that sometimes seems to link a new pilot's voice box to the microphone switch—turn on the latter and you turn off the former. In a few rare cases there is a psychological problem, but ordinary, everyday mike fright can be overcome by practicing the age-old admonition to "always make sure your mind is in gear before engaging your mouth." Nine out of ten IFR communications today consist simply of letting someone know who you are, where you are, and what you want to do; radar takes care of the rest.

Once you get that coveted rating, you'll be glad that the pilots who objected on grounds of required currency stays out of the IFR skies. There's absolutely no way to stay sharp by flying just the legal six hours of instrument time every six months, and for the most part the people who holler about proficiency requirements are the ones who know they can't perform. If you *use* your instrument rating, you'll more than meet the minimums—who says the six hours has to be flown inside a cloud? That's why they make hoods.

Safety Last

It's still the most important part of any kind of flying, but safety couldn't very well have been listed as one of the reasons for not getting an instrument rating. But it will be an effective *pièce de résistance* now that we've bolstered the case for more training.

Whenever the insurance companies get into the act with reduced rates, you can bet they've had their actuaries working to determine how much safer you are likely to be as an instrument pilot. Of course, your fate depends rather heavily on your own actions and procedures and limits, but statistically you're a safer pilot by virtue of the IFR training you receive. You'll be a better all-around pilot with the techniques of instrument flight smoothing and improving every operation. You'll pay more attention to what's going on, and whether you realize it or not, there will be a bit more discipline in your flying — if you've been taught right, you'll fly by the numbers from now on.

And you number sixes, the ones who have no need for the gauges, fly to your hearts' content whenever the skies are fair. If the weather won't let you off the ground, sit around the pilots' lounge and tell lies — and if the hand of government falls heavy on your airspace and begins to restrict it unfairly, so that you *can't* go out on a fair-weather afternoon and do your aviation thing, get out the typewriter and start talking — that's what congressmen are for.

Glossary
Selected Aviation Terms

ADF / Automatic Direction Finder: A low-frequency radio receiver that, when properly tuned, indicates the relative bearing of a non-directional beacon.

AGL / Above Ground Level: An altitude term used to indicate the height of cloud layers and obstructions to flight.

AIRMET / A weather advisory about conditions which will affect primarily lightplane operations, and which will generally require the use of instrument flight rules (IFR).

Altimeter setting / Information available from all ATC facilities to update your altimeter reading to the current atmospheric pressure. Always expressed in inches of mercury.

Approach Control / The ATC facility charged with IFR traffic separation in a terminal area. Approach Control will take over for the final stages of an emergency radar approach to an airport.

ARTCC / Air Route Traffic Control Center: Shortened to "Center" for communications purposes, these facilities are primarily responsible for IFR separation during the enroute phase of a flight. Center's services are also available to other air traffic on a workload-permitting basis, or in an emergency.

ASR / Airport Surveillance Radar: Provides controllers with a radar picture of terminal-area traffic, and can be used to line you up with the final approach course to a runway.

ATC / Air Traffic Control: The entire system of facilities involved in the movement of airplanes in controlled airspace.

Azimuth / A position measured in angular degrees. Used in aviation to specify the relation of an aircraft to a radio station or a radar site.

Bearing / The position of an object or radio station stated in terms of azimuth. Can be either to or from the object or aircraft.

CDI / Course Deviation Indicator: The left-right needle of the VOR display.

Cell / When used in conjunction with a radar advisory or report, implies an area of concentrated precipitation, and *usually* indicates a thunderstorm. To stay on the safe side, always consider a reported cell as a thunderstorm, and request vectors around it.

Ceiling / The lowest cloud layer that covers enough of the sky to be classified as broken or overcast. A non-instrument rated pilot may not legally fly through cloud cover so designated.

Class C Airspace / Airspace (usually cylindrical in shape) around and above an airport with an operating, radar-equipped control tower. This is sacred territory when the weather is less than 1,000 and 3. You have no business flying in Class C airspace without a clearance—besides being hazardous, it's against the law.

Class D Airspace / Generally the same as Class C airspace, except the tower has no radar.

Clearance / Authorization from an ATC facility to proceed through or within or out of the airspace over which control is exercised.

Controlled airspace / A catchall to specify any airspace over which ATC has responsibility for traffic separation when the weather drops below VFR minimums. You may not then fly in controlled airspace unless you have been issued a clearance. (Class A, B, C, D, and E airspace.)

Course / Same as "track," or the imaginary line across the surface of the ground that describes the actual path made good by your airplane.

DF / Direction Finder: The means by which an appropriately equipped ATC facility can determine where you are solely on the basis of your radio transmissions. If all else fails, you can be given vectors to an airport based on the DF information.

Distress / A condition in which you are threatened by serious or imminent danger, and which requires immediate assistance. A non-instrument pilot without normal outside visual clues must be considered "in distress."

Fix / The intersection of any two lines of position, obtained from VOR radial information, DF information or visual sightings, that enables you to say "I am *here*."

Flight Service Station (FSS) / An ATC facility whose primary job is to provide preflight and inflight weather briefings, process flight-plan requests, and respond to pilot requests for information. They are also set up to provide emergency navigational assistance.

Heading / The direction an airplane is pointed, expressed in angular degrees measured from magnetic north. Same as "course" or "track" when there is no wind correction.

Hypoxia / A physiological condition arising from the lack of sufficient oxygen to perform normal functions. Suffered in varying intensity by almost everyone when flying at altitudes above 10,000 feet MSL, and capable of derogating judgment and skill so insidiously that the pilot will be in trouble without being aware of the problem.

Ident / That function of a radar transponder which causes a distinctive image to appear on the radar screen. When a pilot is asked to "squawk ident," just a touch of the button on the transponder does the job.

IFR / Instrument Flight Rules: The set of regulations covering operations under less-than-visual conditions; also, a general term applied to all instrument operations.

ILS / Instrument Landing System: A combination of electronic components that furnishes information in all three dimensions (lateral, longitudinal, and vertical), designed to lead an aircraft to a point very close to the runway.

Localizer / The course guidance signal of an ILS. Activates the left-right needle (CDI) on a VOR display.

Mayday / The international distress code word. When you holler "Mayday" on the radio, everyone who hears you will know that you are in deep trouble and will provide whatever assistance they can.

MSL / Mean Sea Level: The average between high and low tides, and the standard to which most flight altitudes are referenced.

OBS / Omni Bearing Selector: The means of selecting a particular radial or course on a VOR display for subsequent interpretation.

Pilot in Command / The pilot who is responsible for the operation and safety of an aircraft during flight time.

Practice Instrument Approach / An instrument approach procedure (either published or innovative) conducted solely for the purpose of pilot training.

Radar / An acronym for **r**adio **d**etection **a**nd **r**anging, a system which provides to a controller the range and azimuth, and in some cases, the altitude of an aircraft.

Radar contact / The phrase used by controllers to let the pilot know that the radar image on his screen has been positively identified, and that radar service will be continued until the pilot is advised otherwise.

Radar contact lost / The phrase used by controllers to let a pilot know that the aircraft is no longer identifiable on the radarscope, and that whatever radar services were being provided have ceased.

Radial / A magnetic course away from a VOR transmitter. *All* VOR course information is expressed in terms of radials.

Range / The distance of an aircraft from or to something.

Say again / "Please repeat what you just said."

Say again slow / When communications are coming at you from the ground at a rate you can't handle, use of this phrase will reduce that rate considerably. Don't hesitate to use it when things are happening faster than you'd like.

SIGMET / **Sig**nificant **met**eorological advisory. Like an AIRMET, a warning of hazardous weather conditions, but, unlike an AIRMET, this one refers to *severe* weather—thunderstorms, hail, very high winds, etc.

Spatial disorientation / Any condition in which a pilot is unaware of his attitude and/or movement with relation to the earth.

Special VFR / A clearance from ATC to operate into, out of, or through Class C or D airspace as long as you can see a mile and remain clear of clouds. At night, a special VFR clearance is available only to instrument-rated pilots.

Stand by / In radio communications, "wait a minute."

Track / An airplane's actual path across the ground.

Transponder / An avionics unit mounted in an aircraft, and capable of receiving and responding to radar signals from the ground. Transponder-equipped aircraft can be positively identified by ATC controllers.

Transponder code / The sequence of numbers you set in the transponder to provide the desired radarscreen display. Controllers will request aircraft they're working to "squawk" a discrete four-digit code for positive identification.

Uncontrolled airspace / Those portions of the national airspace system over which ATC has no jurisdiction. VFR or IFR, you're on your own in uncontrolled airspace.

Vector / A direction to fly (heading) based on a radar controller's observation of your position. Vectors may aim you toward an airport or away from other traffic, and can line you up with the centerline of a runway at an airport equipped with airport surveillance radar (ASR).

Vertigo / Dizziness caused by spatial disorientation. Vertigo may proceed to incapacitation in some situations. It is usually the end result of an untrained pilot's venture into the clouds.

VFR / Visual Flight Rules: Those parts of the regulations which pertain to flight operations when weather conditions are at or above certain minima. Also generally used to describe any type of visual flight operation.

VOT / VOR Test facility: A VOR transmitter to be used only for checking the accuracy of VOR receivers. It transmits only one radial—360—and a VOR receiver must line up within plus or minus 4 degrees to be considered accurate enough for IFR flight.

Index

About the Author

Richard L. Taylor, award-winning author of many articles and 14 aviation books, writes from a background of continuous pilot activity since 1955, when he entered USAF pilot training. He retired from the Air Force Reserve as a major in 1979, having earned Command Pilot status.

Taylor was for 22 years a member of the aviation faculty at the Ohio State University (now associate professor emeritus), where he was director of flight operations and training and taught at all levels of the flight curriculum. He is the founder and editor of *The Pilot's Audio Update*, a monthly audio tape cassette service published continuously since 1978.

Taylor has accumulated nearly 12,000 hours of pilot time in a wide variety of aircraft including gliders, helicopters, amphibians, turboprops, jets, and most general aviation light airplanes. He remains active as a pilot and an aviation consultant in Dublin, Ohio.